The barn has been born again. A new generation of sympathetic, sensitive barn conversions has been at the forefront of contemporary architecture's push into the countryside. Gone are the clumsy chintz and cartwheel conversions of the 1970s and 1980s and in their place come a new breed of barn houses, as sophisticated and flexible as their urban loft equivalents.

Like the city loft, these barns have rich opportunities for a far more modern way of living than any traditional Victorian or Georgian house could offer. They have wide, open spaces and high dramatic ceilings that suit the current demand for openplan living and room to roam. They have a fluidity and flexibility that allows the natural creation of multifunctional spaces for eating, sitting, relaxing and entertaining. At the same time, barns come with a unique character and charm that flows from their organic simplicity, their unpretentious beauty.

Barns are tied to history and to the landscape and have nothing to hide: they candidly reveal their workings and craftsmanship to anyone who cares to look. In the best conversions old and new come together and offer rich contrasts between vintage materials like oak beams, brick or flint, clapboard or thatch and vibrantly new materials like polished steel and terrazzo, Corian, concrete and chrome. They introduce a wealth of light, which enables a real appreciation of the textures and grandeur of scale within a barn; they play with subtle combinations of vernacular traditionalism and inventive modernity.

The new generation of conversions seeks to ensure they preserve the very qualities of a barn that draw us to them in the first place: the sense of space and scale, the understated elegance of the exteriors and internal framework, as well as the way they nestle naturally into their surroundings. But at the same time, they offer such obvious and enticing potential to shape and mold the interiors in an individual, customized and sometimes unconventional way that mirrors the exact way you want to live your life. Some will seek to live in a barn simply as little more than one large room; others will look for ways and means of lightly shaping the space, perhaps with the use of additions and extensions, to create a blend of more open, public spaces and more intimate, private areas while maintaining the drama of the barn's intrinsic scale. Either way, barns have the sense of an empty theater or stage upon which you can make your own

mark and imprint your own personality, even with the lightest of touches. There is a sense of liberation in the freedom of space and in the freedom of expression.

In particular, barns are proving a haven for an increasing number of city dwellers fleeing the demands of urban life and taking to the country. They take with them a marked design consciousness and a desire to live in contemporary, flexible spaces, which barns can so readily provide. Barn conversions have become second or vacation homes to many who own lofts or converted houses in cities, or they have been taken up as primary homes by an increasing number of people who have tired of the rat race altogether, cashed in on their valuable city property and "downshifted" to simplify and de-stress their lives with a calmer, countryside existence. Knowing only too well the pressures and limitations on space in large towns and cities, these are the kinds of converters who appreciate more than most the grandeur and generosity of space within barns.

"You almost need to have lived in an apartment to realize how precious space is," says Alexander Greenwood of the New Jersey Barn Company, which specializes in the restoration and conversion of old barns. "Most of our clients have been urban people who have lived in the city, perhaps in a loft. At the point they look to get a country house, they don't want all those walls and doors of a farmhouse. They want a more contemporary space and barns can give you that, but the existing materials are still traditional and time worn and wonderful."

Most of the owners of the barns featured in this book have other homes in the city or have lived in the city but thrown in the towel in favor of rural living. Given the difficulties in many regions of building new homes in rural locations—or of finding other houses that offer any real opportunity for flexible living or easy conversion—adapting barns is an obvious solution for this particular kind of ex-urbanite or for anyone seeking a similar way of ordering themselves and their home space.

At the same time, old barns are an available asset. On most farmsteads the older traditional barns have become impractical, as they are mostly unable to cope with large farm machinery and the sheer scale of modern agriculture and its trappings. In my own rural part of England, I see even on the edges of my village vast new agricultural sheds standing right next to crumbling

OPPOSITE **The heart of the Jones House near Nerstrand, Southern Minnesota. This new-build home and contemporary working farm by architect David Salmela draws on the barn and traditional farmstead aesthetic.**

brick, timber and flint barns from the nineteenth century, which are now superfluous. Farther out in the countryside, barns in more isolated locations are especially vulnerable. Sometimes storage barns would be placed away from the farmsteads and between a network of fields. It is these barns that planners might be particularly reluctant to see converted as homes, given their remote settings and lack of services—as well as the ongoing pressure to protect green belts and limit greenfield development—yet it is these buildings that are at special risk of dereliction and collapse.

With falling agricultural revenues and shrinking profits, many farmers are anxious to find new sources of income. Some have converted the disused barns on their own land as holiday cottages, rental homes or farm shops to boost their finances. Many others have sought planning consent for conversions and sold off redundant barns for spiralling amounts, as the demand for barns gradually increased and climbed. As modern farming goes through a harsh, hard process of rationalization, amalgamation and consolidation, many farms have been sold off completely, especially smaller, less profitable farmsteads. In Britain it is thought that recently as many as 1,000 farms a year are sold off and as many as two-thirds of these are being bought by non-farmers. The land might be leased out to contract farmers, the farmhouse adopted and barns converted into additional houses or vacation apartments. Increasingly, developers have their eye on barns and especially small-scale farmsteads, where they might be able to create a small compound of houses from the old barns, outbuildings and the farmhouse itself. Twenty-five years ago, farmers might have seen their decaying, excess barns as a burden, and over the past fifty years many have been demolished and destroyed. Now they are a prize.

At the same time, there has been a general shift among homeowners in cities and country alike towards maximizing all available space. In the countryside this has led to many people looking at outbuildings, coach houses, stables and—with larger period homes, estates or perhaps former rectories that would have needed storage for tithe crops and grain—old barns with a fresh eye, recognizing their value and attraction. The increasing trend towards working from home has led many to convert these spaces into home offices, but they have also been turned into guest lodges and buildings for swimming pools and fitness centers. Again, the sheer flexibility and convention-defying nature of the barn opens up so many possibilities.

This lack of conventionality, the bohemian idea of living in an untraditional space, plus the ideal of a large, theatrical empty space to be molded at will, ties the history of barn conversions to their urban, industrial cousins. Lofts, of course, originated in mostly nineteenth-century buildings where their large, open light-industrial spaces were once used as sweatshops and storage areas by garment businesses, furniture-makers, laundry houses and printers. In New York, especially, some of these iron-framed buildings were colonized in the 1950s by artists looking for live-and-work studio homes as the traditional light industry began moving out of Manhattan to cheaper areas beyond the island. Attracted by low to negligible rents, painters and photographers famously created openplan, multifunction rooms—a studio at one end and a bed and perhaps a kitchenette at the other. Loft living was born, with an emphasis on informality and adaptability that was completely in tune with the increasing frustration with outdated ways of living in traditional homes, where formal dining rooms were never used and claustrophobia ruled.

At the same time, a parallel movement was taking hold out on Long Island, especially in the Hamptons, which has long been a hotbed of creativity, innovative architecture and design. Here, in the 1950s and 1960s, some of those same artists and photographers who were unknowingly inventing the ideal of loft life in the city were also renting out or buying up old potato barns, cart sheds and dairy barns and turning them into summer studios. Roy Lichtenstein settled on a carriage barn in Southampton. Jackson Pollock had a farmhouse with his famous painting barn just behind it. And then there were others like Franz Kline and Robert Dash who took to the barn studio, Dash in a rundown 1740s barn made of reclaimed ships' timbers.

"The barn is a natural studio," says artist Bryan Hunt, who lives in a Tribeca loft in New York and also a small compound consisting of a large eighteenth-century barn, secondary barn house and an ex-chicken coop that connects the two, out in the Hamptons. "Being an artist what you want is a sense of volume and space and what's

BELOW LEFT The stables at the Steffen House, near Salzburg in Austria—a contemporary farmstead designed by architect Heide Mühlfellner—are part of a complex of buildings, including a new barn-like house, built alongside an existing traditional farmhouse. RIGHT One of a number of barns, workshops and outbuildings at the Hancock Shaker Village in the Berkshire Hills of western Massachusetts; the Shaker community was founded in the late eighteenth century. BELOW RIGHT The exterior of a seventeenth-century mill barn in Chargey-Lès-Port, France, converted into a home by Barone Pottgiesser Architects.

OPPOSITE **Artist Bryan Hunt's barn home is in the Hamptons, Long Island. The generously volumed main barn is 200 years old and used, with additional glazing to the front, as Hunt's studio, with bedrooms and bathrooms set off to one side.**
BELOW **A smaller barn forms Hunt's openplan kitchen, dining and living space. A converted chicken coop connects this building to the studio, while all are set within a large garden populated with Hunt's sculptures and sloping down to the shore of the nearby creek.**

wonderful about a barn—like a loft—is that it's a given space that you just work yourself into. Everything is possible within that box, which has a given history and a soul. You are just someone in a long line of occupants or owners and that makes it more interesting and fulfilling."

Today, as well as Bryan Hunt, artist Chuck Close works in a converted barn in the Hamptons, while Jack Youngerman and his wife, Hilary Helfant, have a pair of red barns, one for him and one for her. Donald Baechler has a vintage 45m (150ft) potato barn, sunk into the soil, while out in Montauk playwright Edward Albee runs a foundation for writers and artists in an old converted carriage house known as "The Barn."

Not that all early conversions have to be dappled with the spilled, bright paint of bohemians. Elric Endersby of the New Jersey Barn Company, which has been in business for the past 25 years or so, sees conversions as a relatively recent development, but does know of some examples stretching back 100 years in New England. "It could well be that the movement in the States started in New England where there were a lot

of farms that were left behind as settlement moved west and in outposts where agriculture became redundant. Those were the same areas where in the late nineteenth century the more affluent began to go and create vacation retreats. Barns in those areas were moderately sized because the farms were small, and since they weren't being used it seems natural that they might have been adopted for things like studios, work rooms and then summer rooms. Sooner or later that would lead people to think that these were great spaces, and since they didn't need to be heated in summer you could have a hammock in a corner and a bedstead in the loft, and that's the sort of thing that led people to see the potential of these buildings as houses."

In Britain and some parts of Europe, as in the States, the stock of older and smaller barns was increasingly redundant to farmers, certainly by the 1950s, when large-scale mechanization was becoming widespread and, no matter how hard you tried, a brand-new Massey Ferguson or John Deere combine-harvester would never squeeze through those old cart doors. In the 1950s and 1960s many barns were torn down to make way for newer, larger structures while others fell into disrepair. By the 1970s, conversion was being seen as a positive way of recycling these old buildings and saving them from collapse. Some were turned into museums, theaters, community centers and offices for rural businesses, but most were converted into houses.

For the early converters especially, it was partly the romantic associations of the barn and its ties to the past and to the landscape that attracted them to adapting these buildings into homes. The connotations of barns are, after all, mainly positive in terms of their setting, craftsmanship, space, character, materials and texture. In *Between the Acts* (1941), Virginia Woolf compares a farmyard barn to a temple: "The roof was weathered red-orange; and inside it was a hollow hall, sun-shafted, brown, smelling of corn, dark when the doors were shut, but splendidly illuminated when the doors at the end stood open, as they did to let the wagons in …" Thomas Hardy, in *Far From the Madding Crowd* (1874), compares barns favorably to churches, writing: "The vast porches at its sides, lofty enough to admit a wagon laden to its highest with corn in the sheaf, were spanned by heavy-pointed arches of stone, broadly and boldly cut, whose

very simplicity was the origin of a grandeur not apparent in erections where more ornament has been attempted."

Unfortunately, many barn conversions carried out in the 1970s and 1980s managed to destroy the very things that made barns so alluring in the first place. There was an amateurish spirit to these conversions, where the stated aim of creating a home led owners, architects and builders to turn the barn into a traditional house, with all the baggage that they bring with them. Barns were carved up wholesale and subdivided, destroying the open volume and grand proportions of the space in the quest to create the maximum number of bedrooms, along with familiar rooms for dining, sitting, cooking. Incongruous fireplaces and staircases were grafted on, windows cut into the roof thoughtlessly, and all that was left of the original structure were a few exposed beams here and there. What was a barn had become a house just as traditional and tired as its Victorian neighbor.

These early conversions, as well as poor contemporary equivalents, led conservationists and planning officers to question the wisdom of such projects. The aim was to recycle these valuable rural buildings, to save them from dereliction, to see them sensitively adapted into homes with a minimum of outward change. But if barns were simply being broken up and turned into pastiche houses, within and without, what was the point of it all? These important buildings were not being protected and preserved, after all. They were being vandalized.

No wonder, perhaps, that in some regions planning officers now have a marked antipathy to residential conversions, often preferring less obtrusive conversions for alternative business use that might also generate local employment. Restrictions on conversions can be very tight, especially in conservation areas, and if the building has listed or protected status. In other areas you may be able to do almost anything you like. Either way, planning rules are now minefields that have to be mapped right from the start, before you even commit to buying or taking on a barn. It is sensible to consult local planning authorities, an architect, a surveyor and quite possibly your accountant before signing up for anything, given the facts that virgin barns in themselves are now increasingly expensive, that some have major structural problems and challenges, and that it may well be cheaper in the long run to build a house from scratch.

But, far more positively, it has to be said that the new generation of barn conversions, of a kind featured in this book, is much more in tune with the concerns of conservationists and planning purists, adopting a sensitive, open-minded and sympathetic approach to some wonderful and individual character buildings. Today it is understood that the charm of a barn lies in its proportions and flexibility, its simplicity and rawness. Most architects and owners want large openplan spaces that are suited to contemporary living, where kitchen, dining and living areas are usually combined and only the more private spaces for sleeping and bathing are sectioned off. They also want to preserve the integrity and beauty of the exterior and the barn's surroundings. The new generation conversion is about adopting a light touch, taking a minimal approach that preserves the glories of the barn yet creates an individual, custom-made and contemporary living space.

"The desire to live in these things is partly to do with the fact that they are not like houses," says architect Hans Klaentschi, who built himself a modern barn in Wiltshire, England, for his home and office. "They have a promise of scale and space far beyond an idiotic terraced house. As a generic type the barn form is a very beautiful thing."

Klaentschi is one of an ever increasing number of contemporary architects who have become fascinated not only with vernacular architecture generally, but the form and structure of the barn in particular. Hugh Newell Jacobsen, James Gorst, Anthony Hudson, John Pawson, Kathryn Findlay, Helmut Dietrich, David Salmela and Joe Levine, among others, have found a contemporary resonance within the simplicity and powerful honesty of the barn and its design. Some have contented themselves with conversion, while experimenting with new materials and inspired interventions. Others have taken the barn as a point of inspiration and departure for barn-like houses that draw upon and adapt their proportions, vernacular detailing and organic qualities as well as the way they sit comfortably within the environment. These reinventions and reinterpretations are as much the subject of this book as conversions. Both suggest a way of living that can be highly contemporary yet respect the surrounding environment. The most natural and simple of structures, barns can teach us more than you might expect.

BELOW LEFT **The Steffen House near Salzburg in Austria was designed by Heide Mühlfellner for horse breeders Sigrid and Karl-Heinz Steffen. The exterior is clad in local larch wood.** RIGHT **Timber is the organic unifying material in this converted barn in Lech, Austria, owned by Gerold Schneider and Katia Polletin.** BELOW RIGHT **The open-ended rear of architect Hans Klaentschi's own home, the Long Barn, in Wiltshire, England. This multifunctional part of the contemporary barn house acts as entrance hall, summer room and store.**

13

CHAPTER ONE

LANDSCAPE

There is something childlike about our affection for the barn. These buildings are the simple stuff of children's picture books and *Little House on the Prairie* episodes, where barns tend to be places of escape and refuge. It is similar to the romanticism surrounding barns, centered on their ties to the past, to the days of harvesting by hand and dust in the air over the threshing floor. They seem to be reassuring and solid, fixed and natural.

There is little wonder then that as children we were tempted so easily into the barn, impressed by the great proportions and liberty of this other world. From a child's perspective the emptiness and scale of the barn become all the more impressive and memorable. It is an empty stage for fantasy and play. Hay bales become something for jumping and rolling upon, beams become a climbing frame. In some countries presents would be placed in the barn around Christmas time and some of the animals garlanded, recalling the part of the stable in the Nativity. Our memories are romantic and fond, the associations with the farmyard positive and comforting.

"In the South, where I grew up," says American architect Preston T. Phillips, "the barns had tin roofs painted silver

and after the painting was done, we'd go and collect up silver rocks from where the paint had dripped down on them and bury them in the garden as treasure."

"As a child my first architectural epiphany was when I was about six years old. I remember standing on my own in the neighboring farmer's enormous sixteenth-century thatched barn and the sun coming through a hole in the roof and slanting down and all the particles of dust being caught in this beam," says James Gorst, English architect of the award-winning barn house Whithurst Park Cottage in West Sussex. "Who knows, maybe that was my first moment of wonder?"

Part of the childlike appeal of barns, and part of the reason we have such fond memories, is the way these buildings are so tied into the landscape and their surroundings. They are bold, tactile structures that have a real connection to the land, often seeming to flow or emerge from the ground itself. This is especially true of bank barns, where the structure is built into a bank or hillside, usually with two large ports of entry. The one at basement level, to the front, is at the lowest point of the building, and another farther up the hillside, to the side,

OPPOSITE **A large stone barn and a smaller farmhouse nestle in the open Lancashire moors, north of Bolton, England.**
BELOW LEFT **A view across the fields towards the Jones farmstead, Southern Minnesota, shows how naturally settled it is in the undulating hills.**

RIGHT **A covered bridge over the Housatonic River at Cornwall, Litchfield County, Connecticut, echoes the look of the red barns found near by.**
BELOW RIGHT **This barn and watering hole are in Fauquier County, Virginia, a place of rolling hills and verdant woodland.**

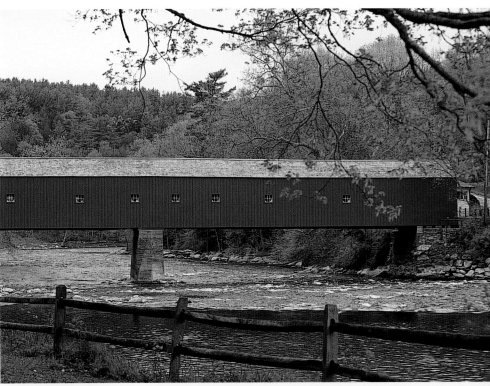

is at first-floor level; this is sometimes accessed via a gentle ramp. The lower level would usually have been for the animals and the upper levels used for storage and threshing. Building the barn in this way offered good and generous access to two different parts of the barn at once, maximizing its flexibility and convenience. Potato barns, too, were partly sunken into the ground to provide cool storage, while other agricultural structures —such as hatcheries—also hug the ground and seek protection from their surroundings.

Practically, barns needed a symbiotic relationship with the land. It had to be possible to get animals, carts and people in and out of a barn without a struggle. The barn had to be well positioned for access and to shield it from the elements, from the rain, from the wind. That might mean a barn nestling into the side, or just over the brow, of a hill, the farmer using the natural contours of the land to offer his building valuable protection.

"Historically, the barn had to connect easily to the landscape and there wasn't the money to spend on structural gymnastics," says Jeff Dreyfus, an architect based in Charlottesville, Virginia, who is much influenced by the local vernacular, and especially the form of farm compounds. "The barn had to work with the land and be open to it. There needs to be a big opening for getting in and out, ventilation if you want it, and there's an honesty to the roofs, which are there simply to shed water and to provide shade. They are not confusing buildings at all; they are very straightforward."

The materials used to construct a barn—local stone, timber, brick or flint from the surrounding forests and fields—tied it to its immediate environment. There were many variations on the form of the barn, according to its function, even though most shared basic principles of openness and box-like simplicity. There were cart barns and granaries, cow sheds and dairies, stables and hatcheries, all tied to the necessities and needs of the farmer. But there were also many multifunctional barns, where you might have animals on one level, a threshing floor on another and storage above or to the sides for carts, hay or grain. A simple barn structure could easily accommodate many purposes and uses.

Yet by the nineteenth century, farms were already beginning to be overtaken by change. The wholesale mechanization and industrialization of farming started

OPPOSITE **The exterior of the Spencer Barn, near Spooner, Wisconsin, by Alchemy Architects, merging with the woods. The look of the house was partly inspired by the cover of the American children's book *My Cousin Katie*, with its red barns and farm buildings.**

BELOW **This simple Alpine barn is set in the country-side around Lech, Austria.**
BOTTOM **A converted English stone barn in Lancashire, by Evans Vettori Architects. The new large bay window to the front of the building is a purposeful addition, creating a distinct contrast between old and new.**

to shift the scale of production and also the buildings needed to house the machinery and detritus of it all. The first mechanical harvesters and steam-driven threshing machines were coming into use by the 1860s. Already, a harvest was becoming a process of weeks rather than months, of few rather than hundreds of laborers. By the 1930s tractors were in mass production and by the 1950s so were combine-harvesters. Cart and plough horses were redundant, as were many of their masters. The stables emptied, and threshing floors became useless. In North America in the 1870s, as many as 85 out of 100 people lived on a farm. But by the 1970s it was down to 15.

In the new era of the instant harvest, period barns became vulnerable. Some were torn down to make way for new, larger agricultural sheds, which could be used to house combine harvesters and tractors. Others were neglected, and relegated in use. Many barns simply began to crumble back into the landscape that had given them life in the first case, often replaced by more incongruous, industrial-looking buildings.

"We were appalled that wonderful buildings that had required so much effort to construct in the first place were being pushed over and hauled away to landfill," says Alexander Greenwood of the New Jersey Barn Company. "There was no effort, especially by developers, to make use of what already existed on the landscape. In many cases they removed what seemed appropriate—a building that was an organic thing made of timber and stone—and replaced it with something very alien."

A large part of the allure of barn conversions is now linked into the fact that barns tend to be so well keyed into the landscape. The locations are usually rural and appealing, often set on the edge of villages or small settlements, away from busy roads and built-up areas. The surroundings, naturally, tend to be farmland with views of fields and grazing pastures, though you might have to share your driveway with a tractor and its trailer. Researching potential drawbacks of living in conversions situated close to or on working farms is a very good idea before taking on a conversion project, as you may find that the mass-production aspects of modern farming and its associated machinery do not always fit well with your dream of a tranquil country existence.

Sensitive conversions usually respect the ties that a building has to the landscape, working with sympathetic materials on the one hand but also respecting and conserving the immediate surroundings on the other. First and foremost, a barn really needs room to breathe, to be seen in the context of the land. There is a real sense of drama and beauty to a barn alone in a field or meadow, sitting within the contours of the land. Yet many developers tend to curtail the curtilage of a barn, enclosing it within small suburban-like plots, fenced in and forced to subsist in an impoverished setting. A suburban approach to landscaping, introducing tarmac or paved driveways, obtrusive outbuildings and the other trappings of everyday gardens, can also seem very out of place when allied to a barn.

As with the barn itself, the most successful approach to the context of the building seems to be to adopt the lightest of touches. Many of the projects in this book avoid formal gardens altogether, simply encircling the barn house with meadowlands and wild flowers. The more cultivated elements are tucked away and contained, creating a very informal and natural setting. The trees and grassland become a kind of wild garden, often tying in with surrounding farmland and fields. At the same time, essentials like oil tanks, drainage and services are hidden as much as possible, reducing the visual mess around the barn. The mesmeric simplicity of the line and form of the barn almost demands it, asking to remain unbroken. The garage might be a barn-like building in itself, giving the feel of a farm compound and echoing the main building, while driveways are little more than farm tracks or gravel roads.

The best contemporary architects and designers have learned many lessons from the way barn structures and farm buildings sit within and relate to the landscape around them. These are buildings that seek to connect with the landscape and sustain a relationship with it, rather than rudely intruding upon it or trying to make a statement that runs contrary to the land. Partly this has been through using materials and vernacular methods of building, belonging to the locality, but it has also involved architects looking more closely at how they site their buildings in the landscape around them. The barn teaches respect for its environs and many contemporary new-build barn houses, such as the Innfeld House (see pages 30–7), or James Gorst's Whithurst Park Cottage in West Sussex (see pages 48–55), follow that lesson.

The Innfeld House is lightly placed on the slopes of an Austrian hillside, alongside other barns and agricultural buildings, so it almost becomes one part of a farm compound, surrounded by grassland. Gorst's building nestles into the trees and forestry to the rear, while overlooking pasture and grazing fields.

Both contemporary conversions and new-build barn houses seek to create connections between the interiors and the landscape outside, establishing some degree of transparency between the two. With conversions, where the whole issue of glazing and light can be particularly problematic, this transparency usually comes through large sections of glazing within the immense barn door entrance areas. Sometimes the barn will have twin doors at opposite sides of the barn that can both be glazed, introducing a strong level of transparency that almost allows the landscape to pass between the two.

New-build houses offer more opportunities to play with the whole issue of transparency and provide strong connections between inside and out. Many buildings, such as Gorst's Whithurst Park Cottage, use sheets of glazing on the lower levels to create transparency and slide the eye out into the surroundings. One's gaze is constantly drawn outwards, taking advantage of the rich setting, rather than bouncing off featureless walls. This transparency seems to open up the volumes of the space, playing visual tricks, as well as revealing and framing picture-book vistas of the exteriors beyond. Unlike many more traditional houses, these barn homes make the most of their country setting and innovate to achieve this symbiosis in terms of glazing, structural supports and thermal insulation.

At the same time, conversions and new-build barns alike provide a sense of reassurance, tied to the ideal of a barn at one with the land. "There's a visual weight to a barn that gives people comfort," Jeff Dreyfus says. "We all have barns that we know of that may have been built 150 years ago but are still beautiful and still there, even if they are just a shell. There is a sense of permanence to barns literally and in the memory that we don't see in most other buildings these days when shopping malls are being built with a shelf life of 30 years."

OPPOSITE **The open doors of the Conference Barn, near Middleburg, Virginia, lead you out towards the meadows of this working farmstead. The new barn was designed by Sant Architects to echo existing barns and stables near by while adopting its own contemporary aesthetic.**
BELOW LEFT AND RIGHT **At one end of Hans and Paula Klaentschi's Long Barn, in Wiltshire, the partly open walls of the summer room tempt you into the gardens, while at the other sheet glazing in the openplan living/dining room connects inside and out.**

LEVINE BARN

WAYNE COUNTY, PENNSYLVANIA, USA

BY BONE LEVINE ARCHITECTS

Architect Joe Levine's converted nineteenth-century bank barn has a sublime location. It looks out across gently sloping meadow grass towards the valley lands and winding form of the Delaware River; behind is a thick carpet of forestry stretching up the hill, green and lush. The nearby road is little more than a track; barely a single car passes in a morning. You could safely say this is tranquillity. And the barn itself almost slips back into the landscape, unobtrusive and content.

"As a child I came up to summer camp about 45 minutes away from here, so I knew the Delaware River quite well," says Levine, whose practice is based in New York and who uses the barn as a summer and weekend place for himself and his family. "This barn is on a 30-acre property that's owned by some friends of ours who we've known in New York for a long time. When they bought the land they thought they would transform the barn into a house, but built a new home near by instead. They thought the barn was too big a problem. Then the barn started getting into serious shape and they asked me if I wanted it. Site unseen we made a deal."

Some might have pulled the barn down and rebuilt it or started again from scratch, given the building was in such a bad way. Levine knew that if he took it down he would end up replacing so much of the structure that he would risk losing the original character of the place. Dating back to 1840 and primarily used for animal shelter, the barn is rumored to have been a "station" on the underground network used by escaping slaves heading north to the Canadian border; a dug-out area in the basement was supposed to have been the escape hole. The original main floor had collapsed and been replaced by a substitute while the hemlock wood clapboards were falling apart. Most importantly, the roof was buckling and the whole building was starting to slide down the hillside, carried by the slip water flowing off the hills and woodland in heavy rains. This was a building in danger of returning to the earth and elements.

"But when I first walked into the barn, there was something incredible about the proportions of the singular space," says Levine. "Another thing that was

ABOVE **The barn has settled naturally in its surroundings. Materials such as the cedar siding and lead-coated copper roof improve with age and recess the barn farther into the landscape.**

OPPOSITE **A high degree of transparency allows the landscape to flood into the barn; large wooden sliding doors can be opened to allow air, light and view to filter through.**

significant was the way the light came in through the slats in the barn-board siding of the wall. So it was all about trying to capture and maintain the integrity of the space and, as my wife put it, 'If you lose that quality of the light coming in through the slats, you've blown it.'"

The priority was to stabilize the building, both from above and from below. First, split posts and beams were cabled together and clamped, while the main purlins—or horizontal support beams—were braced with large vice-like pieces of equipment. The cabled structure was then slowly raised and straightened by tightening the vices little by little. The joists and rafters were slowly brought back into line and eventually the building was racked back into a stable condition.

Down below, a complex cribbing structure was built to support the base of the barn while new, deep foundation piles were put in, 3.7m (12 ft) deep. The old dug-out area below the main floor was excavated further to create a proper basement area to house essential services, such as the oil tank, boiler and so on, as well as a fully functioning workshop. This workshop then became a nerve center for the restoration of the rest of the house, undertaken by Levine and his new neighbor, cabinet-maker and craftsman Larry Braverman.

Because the post and beam structure of the building was still irregular and out of line, the barn was effectively given a new outer coat of high-performance walls, complete with insulation and water proofing, with a gap of around 60cm (2ft) to the original wall line. "But the original post and beam structure is still completely functioning," Levine explains. "It's still the real support of everything that's here, including the east wall of glass, which has substantial weight and wind loads and is entirely supported back on to the timber frame."

This east wall—the front of the house—features a layer of glazing at the top with another layer of sliding glass doors below that, which can be sheathed and protected by a flexible system of external shutters, made of recycled hemlock wood from the original barn siding. This wall of glazing introduces a high level of transparency, while the light filtering through the gaps in the wooden shutters recalls that first experience of entering the ruined barn and seeing the light filtering through its decaying siding. The glazing opens up the barn to the panoramic landscape beyond, with the soft contours of

OPPOSITE **Two simple and wall-less sleeping platforms have been created at second-floor level, at slightly different heights, which preserve the overall integrity and proportional generosity of the barn.**
ABOVE AND RIGHT **The heart of the barn has been kept largely open, with an uninterrupted sweep from the wooden sliding panels at the front to the double glass doors that lead to the rear terrace.**

the trees flowing alongside the Delaware. The outside comes in and the inside slips out, especially when the glass doors are opened up. At the same time, there are large sheet-glass double doors at the back of the house, leading on to a terrace, with the forestry beyond. With the two sets of glass doors pushed back, light, air and the odd bird can pass through unimpeded.

Inside, the barn has essentially been kept as one large space. "What we have done," says Levine, "is try to maintain the barn as a no-room house. Even the bathroom is more or less a deconstruction—it's just enclosed by storage and closets around it. Privacy is a problem, but it was less of a priority for us than the beauty and integrity of the space. There was one hay loft in the barn originally and that became the genesis for the sleeping platforms. We built two sleeping lofts that hang from the original structure and don't really connect to any walls. We just needed a couple of staircases to reach them, although we used ladders for a year or so."

Materials within the barn mix old and new, but they have a largely organic feel that ties in with the rugged, rural setting. The floors, for instance, are cherry wood and underheated. The ceiling uses the timber of the original barn roof with a new outer layer added on top. The cabinet work is in maple veneer ply, while the floors for the two lofts are in recycled oak and the frames for

windows and doors are made of reclaimed yellow pine. Outside, the original foundation stone walls at the base of the barn are made from the local bluestone, while the new siding is in cedar with a lead-coated copper external roof—both are materials that weather and improve with time, settling back into their surroundings.

The exterior surroundings to the barn have been purposefully kept low key: meadow grass and a simple dirt drive leading up to the house. From a distance the house seems to nestle back into the trees and to hug the landscape. "Barns were strategically situated on the land for functional reasons more than anything," says Levine. "With other landscaping related to farming, grazing and the passing of time, the placement of the barn became so integrated into the site that it eventually becomes one with the surrounding environment."

After five years of work getting the main barn done, the next project is the construction of a small guest "house" near by, using the form of a circular New York timber water tower. "Being out at the barn makes the city seem a much better place," Levine says. "I've pretty much grown to need it. I guess a barn is akin to lofts in New York with large, open spaces. Even opening up our home in Brooklyn didn't provide us with a great deal of space. And the romance of the barn has always been part of our psyche. It's certainly understandable."

INNFELD HOUSE

SCHWARZENBERG, VORARLBERG, AUSTRIA

BY DIETRICH UNTERTRIFALLER ARCHITEKTEN

At the westernmost tip of Austria, bordered closely by Germany to one side and Switzerland to the other, the region of Vorarlberg has established itself as a leading European center for innovative architecture, in both town and country. In rural areas, especially, this region has seen a wealth of experimentation over the past 25 years, and this movement has drawn heavily on vernacular traditions and local craftsmanship.

Based in Bregenz, the architectural practice of Dietrich Untertrifaller has played a leading part in Vorarlberg's drive to innovate and ameliorate, especially when it comes to houses. Helmut Dietrich and Much Untertrifaller's buildings are strongly linked to their surroundings and take into account the importance of local vernacular architecture, patterns of development in rural villages and settlements, and the use of appropriate and sympathetic materials. At the same time, the spirit of their work is decidedly contemporary in application, and it fits in with a way of living that is both modern and more informal yet also pragmatic.

Helmut Dietrich's new design for the Innfeld house in the village of Schwarzenberg demonstrates all the above criteria. It sits within a soft hillside location, with woodland close by. Next door is a period farmhouse, which the new building both respects and flirts with, while assuming its own identity. The Innfeld house draws on the look and finish of a long, rectangular local farmhouse and connected barn – or *Einhaus* – where part of one long, single structure will be for living and part used for farm storage, a pattern fairly typical within Austria, Bavaria and other parts of Germany.

While assuming an aesthetic link with other, neighboring houses, the new barn house also has a strong and important relationship with the landscape itself. Indeed, says Dietrich, this was one of the greatest priorities in designing this family house for his clients, Andreas and Gabriele Innfeld. Like a bank barn, the house burrows into the gentle slope of the hillside, creating a half-length basement level that houses a music room and services below the main first floor. Bedrooms are located on the first floor, while a large

OPPOSITE **Placing the main living spaces at the top of the house and maximizing the glazing to the front elevation offers spectacular picture-book views across the wooded valleys**

ABOVE **The use of timber and the vernacular barn-like form of the building create a natural synergy with the traditional Bregenzerwald house situated near by**

loft-like and mostly openplan living, kitchen and dining area has been created right at the top of the house. Turning the traditional house layout upside down and placing the main living spaces at the top of the house reinforces the connection with the landscape, in the sense that this level is the perfect viewing platform for appreciating the surroundings. The views from all sides of this dramatic room lead you outwards to the countryside, the valley setting and layers of woodland.

On all three different floors of the house, the eye is led out through banks of sheet glazing at the face of the building, looking right down the hillside and maximizing the panorama beyond. But on the top floor vast sliding glass doors also lead to a large covered loggia or veranda cut out from the main body of the house, sitting within the main profile of the roof. Here there is an almost seamless transition between outdoors and in, all on one floor level, creating a choice of indoor and outdoor areas for eating and sitting. Plants, bird tables and deck chairs furnish a semi-enclosed outdoor space where one can closely appreciate the changing seasons and shifting weather patterns.

This multifunctional space is also the most barn-like room in the house, with its high-vaulted ceilings, coated in white fir, and its generous proportions. It is lightly divided not by columns or by solid walls but by low-slung or half-height elements within the space, such as the large island unit that helps delineate the kitchen zone, with a dining area to one side, by the windows. There are also two block-like tiled stoves with flues reaching up into the ceiling, which help separate the space. One low-slung unit lies to one side of the kitchen while the other, more vertical, slab-like unit creates a more solid divider for a more intimate television lounge

ABOVE LEFT AND LEFT **The key rooms in the house all face down the valley, reinforcing the relationship between the barn and its surroundings. The master bedroom has sliding doors with a wooden balcony, while there is a veranda at the top of the house.**

OPPOSITE **As the house weathers, it takes on a patina of age and sinks back naturally into the landscape. Glazed panels introduced in the sides of the building strengthen the feeling of transparency and introduce light to the rear of the building.**

PREVIOUS PAGES:
LEFT In the hallway, a floor-to-ceiling sheet of glass provides a connection with the walnut tree outside and the house beyond.
RIGHT On the top floor there is a choice of dining areas—indoors, or out on the terrace.

RIGHT AND FAR RIGHT
Much of the main living space on the top floor has been kept openplan, with the kitchen and two heating elements partially intersecting the room to one side. To the rear is a more private television/ family room.

that is accessed by a large sliding door with frosted glass. These wood-burning stoves help distribute heat evenly around the house, while also being striking architectural objects in themselves.

The use of materials contrasts intrinsically organic with man-made modern. The shifting textures and grains of the different woods for ceiling and floors, which are made of walnut, reinforce the cabin-like flavor of the house and also tie in with the surroundings—the forestry near by and the tall walnut tree that stands between the new house and the old farmhouse beyond. Sheets of frosted glass used to enclose the wooden stairway that is cantilevered from the main supporting wall, set at one side, act as a child-friendly safety screen, but they also allow light and shadows to filter through. In the master bedroom the bed faces the wall of big windows, with a sliding glass door opening directly on to a slatted wooden balcony. Even on the first floor, in the hallway, a large window frames the walnut tree with a view of the old farmhouse beyond. Each example of such transparency reinforces the barn's connections with the exterior and with the natural environment.

There is a self-contained neatness to the house, with a garage and entrance hall at the back of the house at first-floor level, which in a traditional long, connected barn might have been used for animals or agricultural storage. There is very little in the way of landscaping— little more than a gravel driveway and a thin pathway of shingle surrounding the house. Apart from that, the meadows themselves become a massive, open garden— an unadulterated, rolling setting without fences or obstruction. As the timber cladding weathers over time, it also shifts in color and tone, like the neighboring farmhouses, and ties itself into the passing seasons.

The work of Dietrich Untertrifaller has often drawn on the local vernacular to create compact, elegant houses. They include the Innfeld, Rüscher and Sutterlüty houses, built between 1998 and 1999, which share a distinct aesthetic and look—striking structures with an organic simplicity. They reference the look of farmhouses, barns and alpine cabins, although each is very specific to its particular location and setting. Together they suggest that modern houses designed with thought and subtlety really can be compatible with and sympathetic to the countryside, just as barns always have been.

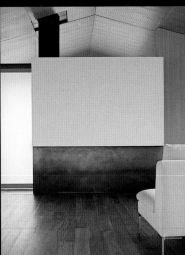

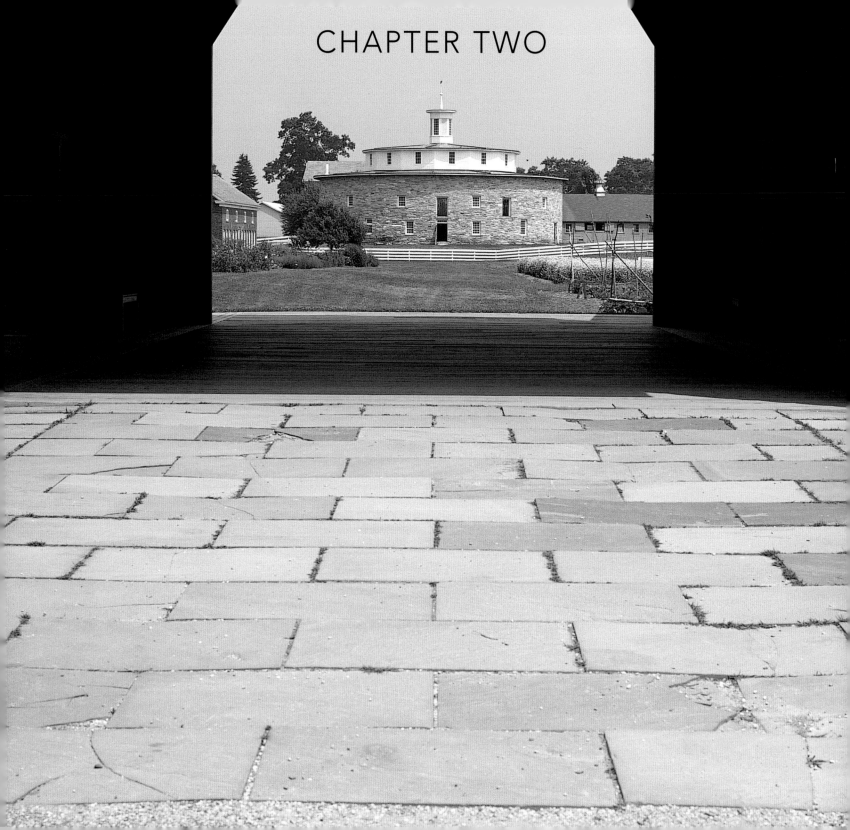

CHAPTER TWO

ARCHITECTURE

To talk of barns is to speak in generalizations. We have a classic picture-book image in our minds of a box-like building with a steeply pitched roof, sitting alone in the landscape with its large double cart doors the only real interruption, gaping open like some hungry mouth. Of course, the story of the barn is far more complex than that. Barns are the most vernacular of buildings, closely tied in to their location, using regional methods of construction as well as incorporating materials gathered from the immediate surroundings. This gives the form and structure of barns a mass of variety and variation, a wealth of differences despite many marked similarities in proportion, scale and intrinsic character.

The architecture of barns shifts from country to country and from state to state, depending on the prevailing vernacular aesthetic. In England even from county to county one sees a great deal of variation, from modest low-slung single-storey barns and stables to soaring, grand structures complete with hay lofts and enormous multifunctional spaces. Traditional village tithe barns were built close to churches and rectories, to be used for storing one tenth of local farmers' crops as a local church "tax." They can exhibit a relative grandeur and scale, but, sadly, by the nineteenth century many were destroyed as tithes began to be paid in cash rather than crops. Monastic barns and barns alongside big period country houses or farm estates were also often built on a grander scale and could take many months or years to construct, despite being governed by familiar principles of simplicity and flexibility, possessing little in the way of decoration or embellishment apart from occasional weathervanes and built-in dovecotes.

In North America the settlers from different parts of Europe brought their various vernacular methods of building with them and they applied them to their new communities. The English or Yankee Barn was perhaps the most common, and this style formed a basis for the evolution of most American barns, particularly in New England. It was generally a straightforward three-bay barn with side access. The Long House, *Einhaus* or Quebec Connected Barn was essentially a house and barn combined, situated at either end of a single rectangular building; it originated in Germany and parts of France and Austria. Whereas the English Barns were characterized by tall supporting walls and steeply pitched roofs, Dutch Barns or New World Dutch Barns tended to have low-slung supporting walls and gently pitched roofs, bringing the whole building closer to the ground, with entrances generally placed at both of the gable ends. Pennsylvania Barns also became common—two-level bank barns, built into the hillside or a slope with entrances at first-floor and basement levels.

But aside from these key generic types, there were countless variations upon a theme. There were no hard and fast rules; these were flexible buildings and could be adapted and altered at will depending on particular need and the scale of local agriculture. The American pioneers tended to build on a much larger scale than their European cousins, suggesting their hope and faith in the American Dream, perhaps, but this upsizing also related to the practicalities of farming on a larger scale or sometimes to the sharing of barns by farmers and communities. Form also followed function, with barns adapted to suit particular purposes or house different kinds of animals. Side aisles might be added away from a threshing floor for cattle or horses. Additions and lean-tos could be glued on as hatcheries or silos.

Sometimes American communities would step away from tradition and try something completely new. The Shakers, in particular, experimented with beautiful but relatively complex round barns. Standing among more familiar barns, houses and meeting halls, the restored round barn found at the Shaker Village in Hancock, Massachusetts, is a fine example of a dramatic and innovative form of building. Striking in its associations with far more modern forms of architecture, it suggests the defensive look of European Martello towers and coastal forts. Built in 1826 in stone and timber, it was conceived as a highly functional building. Cattle were housed at a lower, first-floor or basement level, with its own access points and a subterranean manure store. Above was a wagon level and threshing floor, into which carts could be driven via an earth ramp to navigate the circumference of the building with a 27m (90ft) diameter. At the center of the building was a massive hay store, constructed so that hay could easily be passed down to the cattle below. A dairy wing and twin silos were added later, creating a very efficient farming unit.

Complex, time-consuming and relatively rare, round barns were usually communal structures rather than a

BELOW LEFT AND RIGHT **At the Hancock Shaker Museum, outside Pittsfield, Massachusetts, the Shaker village is dominated by a vast round stone and timber barn that was built in 1826 (see page 38 for an exterior view). With a circumference of 82m (270ft), the barn has a** hay store and threshing floor above and cattle stabling below.

RIGHT **A typical example of a New England working barn found at Old Chatham, Massachusetts, with the main timber-framed building "accessorized" by smaller structures that have been added over the years.**

RIGHT "I wanted a house that echoed this sort of mid-western farm look but was very 'today,'" owner Thad Spencer has said of his new-build barn in Wisconsin, designed by Alchemy Architects. The barn is covered in 1.2 x 2.5m (4 x 8ft) sections of Parklex siding—a resin-impregnated wood.

OPPOSITE ABOVE The glazed doors and windows that run around the bottom section of Sant Architects' Conference Barn in Virginia impart an element of transparency and invite light into the space.

OPPOSITE BELOW The central courtyard of David Salmela's Jones House and farmstead in Minnesota is built to a largely U-shaped pattern consisting of house, granary, guest house and garage.

single farmer's store. They were remarkably beautiful, although more conventional buildings often shared a similar emphasis on craftsmanship and pride in self-achievement. These were instinctive buildings, their methodology passed down through the succeeding generations, shifting and adapting along the way. Some might seek the help of self-build manuals or bring in carpenters and laborers, but the sense of an organic, purposeful, utilitarian structure remained. In the United States, in particular, farmers took pride in their buildings to the extent of sometimes adding decoration such as hex signs, painted on the timber sidings.

The combination of vernacular techniques and the instinctive, intuitive nature of barn buildings did not traditionally endear them to architects, who tended to save themselves for more important concerns. Yet the revival of interest in vernacular architecture that began among the twentieth-century Modernists has gathered pace over recent years. Even in the 1970s and 1980s, commentators were noting the lack of interest among architects in barns and farm buildings and lamenting the continued destruction and dereliction of period barns. But that has now all changed and many contemporary architects have become fascinated with the materials, construction, form and character of the barn, as well as other types of vernacular building.

The simplicity and unpretentious nature of the barn does, after all, offer a pleasing antidote to the visual and architectural excesses of the Post-Modern Movement and the somewhat complex statement made by high tech, computer-aided morphic buildings. "Barns are pure structures," says English architect James Gorst, whose Whithurst Park Cottage in West Sussex is featured on pages 48–55. "I suppose what appeals to architects is the simplicity and purity of a barn. It's a unified thing, a very pure architectural solution."

For a number of contemporary architects interested in converting, recycling and reinventing barns, the buildings have offered themselves up for other, public uses—theaters, museums, art galleries and community centers, for example. Hawkins Brown reinvented the Sheep Field Barn at sculptor Henry Moore's Perry Green estate in Hertfordshire, England, as a striking gallery for Moore's artwork. Bauman Lyons Architects converted three barns at the Yorkshire Sculpture Park, near

Wakefield, as a gallery, studios and cafe. In St. Andrews, Scotland, Nicoll Russell Studios rebuilt and reinvented an old cowshed as the Byre Theatre.

Large existing barns easily lend themselves to such other uses. But architects have also looked to the form and structure of the barn in designing new buildings, particularly in rural locations. These buildings are rooted in vernacular architecture and make use of many traditional materials, especially timber, but they are also very contemporary, vibrant places. There is David Chipperfield's River and Rowing Museum in Henley-on-Thames, Oxfordshire, which looks on one level like a modern equivalent of a boathouse but also has the feel of an Oxfordshire barn. Maya Lin's Langston Hughes Library in Knoxville, Tennessee, has the outward look of a simple timber barn raised up on a modest plinth-like platform. It sits very naturally, like a farm building, within its rural context yet has a very contemporary interior.

Van Heyningen and Haward Architects' visitors center at the Anglo-Saxon archaeological site of Sutton Hoo in Suffolk, England, also adopts the outward appearance of two timber barns, blending well with the woodland and countryside location. And Edward Cullinan's Downland Gridshell building at the Weald and Downland Open Air Museum, near Chichester, West Sussex, uses a fluid timber-frame structure. Almost like an undulating armadillo shell, it looks like a twenty-first-century barn, hugging the landscape, and it serves to reinforce the museum's work, which is rescuing period vernacular, timber-framed buildings.

Yet it is in the design of contemporary houses that we see the most common references to the barn within the work of a broad range of contemporary architects, tied in again to the global revival of interest in vernacular techniques and structures. Swiss architect Peter Zumthor works out of a converted barn studio and has drawn heavily on the look of the Alpine barn in houses such as

the Gugalun House in mountainous Versam, Switzerland. In Australia, Glen Murcutt's Marika Alderton House in the Northern Territory has the appearance of a small barn on stilts, recalling the raised barns you sometimes see in England set up on saddle stones. It is a flexible building, with a series of timber and plywood shutters that can be opened up in the heat of the day to make an almost transparent building. Add to that the work of Turner Brooks, Charles Gwathmey, David Salmela, Hugh Newell Jacobsen and others in the United States, which draws widely on vernacular architecture—barns and farm buildings included—to create contemporary new homes that are set naturally within the landscape.

Andrus Burr, of Burr & McCallum Architects, based in Williamstown, Massachusetts, has drawn on the look of New England farm buildings and barns, as well as that of urban industrial buildings and warehouses, in the design of a number of new houses in the region. Burr & McCallum's Lenox House, near Pittsfield, combines the spacious feeling of a loft with a barn aesthetic, while the whole structure is wrapped in a distinctive vernacular language. The Lenox House takes the form of a small compound of buildings, like a farmyard congregation. "We relied heavily on the barn aesthetic and we have always liked collections of buildings, particularly the way farmers arrange their buildings to form exterior spaces that are protected from the wind but are open to the sunlight," says Burr. "One of the reasons we like barns and industrial buildings is that the interior spaces are big and open and much more like the way people want

RIGHT AND OPPOSITE **Two views of the openplan front section of Burr & McCallum's Lenox House, near Pittsfield, Massachusetts, with its mix of barn and farm aesthetic.**

With its exposed beams and columns, and open roof structure and bare brick walls, this new-build barn has the light-industrial references that one might expect from a loft.

to live now than traditional New England houses. There are many more possibilities for openplan living when you are using utilitarian vernacular."

Such approaches have created a hybridized version of a contemporary barn house. In the worst examples, barn houses have been translated into some very false-looking developer-led buildings that attempt to give the look of a barn conversion in undeniably suburban settings, using cheap and inappropriate materials. But at their architectural best, these new barn homes—as in the work of Burr & McCallum—fuse modern ways of living with vernacular looks and detailing, a thoughtful use of materials and an aesthetic that sits very well within the landscape and in rural settings.

In the UK architect Roderick James and his company Carpenter Oak have specialized in the design and build of barn houses. James started with barn conversions but then began to broaden out into new-build homes that had timber frames, vernacular detailing and barn-like proportions. "When people first come and see us," says James, who works out of a new barn in Devon, "they are

seduced by the simple barn shape, which is easy and comfortable to live with. But we have now moved on to designing houses that have taken the key ingredients of that barn space without following the strict rhythm of bay sizes and proportions. That gives us more flexible buildings, with curving shapes and roofs, for instance. You have got to think very carefully about what you are creating. It's not that difficult to create hard-edged, hard-lined buildings that are obviously modern. The trick is trying to design and produce buildings that have a crispness and a cleanness to them but still which have an organic feeling to them."

From dismissing barns as irrelevant and parochial, modern architecture has come to realize the value of the character, simplicity and spatial generosity of barns. Architects now recognize that barns and barn forms are perfectly suited to many of the lifestyle changes that architecture has been busily responding to, being ideal for the creation of openplan, flexible and multipurpose rooms with a healthy sense of scale. Like lofts, barns were once neglected. Now they are beloved.

OPPOSITE **The exterior of Schneider and Polletin's converted barn in Lech, Austria, which is used as a multifunctional space: a home for visiting artists, a meeting house and a gallery, with the basement set aside for Polletin's architectural office.**
BELOW LEFT **This converted barn in Suffolk, by the English architect James Gorst, was designed as a self-contained annex to the large modernized farmhouse near by.**
BELOW RIGHT **An interior view of a converted barn in Lancashire, England, by Evans Vettori Architects.**

Cottage in the county of West Sussex. Set to one side of extensive parkland, with forestry directly behind it, the house was commissioned as a contemporary guest lodge by clients planning to build a new and much larger country home perched on a hillside some distance away. Gorst wanted to create a building that would have a life and strength of its own, but also be unobtrusive in relation to this unbuilt big brother. The look of a barn seemed the perfect solution, assuming a natural presence in this rural location surrounded by farmland.

"It's a modern barn and refers to barns yet takes the tradition forward," says Gorst. "I didn't want to suburbanize or domesticate the meadows and I didn't want it to look too much like a house at all, or to have anything in the way of formal gardens. I wanted to play up the agricultural side of it and I also wanted an archetypal form, which the barn was. These things help you start the narrative of the building."

Gorst had recently visited Finland and noted how the Finns often site country houses on the thresholds of woods and fields, rather than out in the open. Attracted

BY JAMES GORST ARCHITECTS

THIS PAGE **The central staircase serves to lightly delineate the first floor. At one end of the house lies the openplan kitchen, designed by Gorst in oak and MDF, and the dining area is near by, with a table by Martin van Severin and chairs by Montis.**
OPPOSITE **The surrounding parklands have been preserved, with simple grasses and wild plants. Together with the use of sympathetic materials and the transparency of the first floor, this makes the house feel a part of the existing landscape.**

by the idea of contrasting openness to one side of the building with seclusion to the other, he decided to position the cottage on a spot close beside the trees, with few windows to the rear and its façade looking out across the unspoilt meadow lands.

"The forest is the unknown and sheltering force while the meadow is openness and light," says Gorst. "It's as if the house is hovering between these two worlds and you don't quite know which one it belongs to. I was interested in that as a theme for the house, which carried through to the architecture in the way it is completely glazed at first-floor level and the first floor is where you are in the day with the landscape as your wallpaper. But then the bedrooms upstairs have very few windows and I wanted that to be a much more introspective space that you retire to. That's why the center of the roof is cracked open to let light drop into the center of the building and then go in through internal glazed screens in the stairwell to the bedrooms."

The banks of glazing at low level, as well as the steeply pitched zinc-copper-titanium alloy roof, give a feeling of modernity that is juxtaposed with the very traditional, vernacular flavor of the oak frontage that stretches across the rest of the exterior. The oak panelling was chosen partly to tie in with the barn flavor, and partly because the local area is rich in oak and so it was felt to be a natural choice. But it was also chosen because the wood will slowly turn gray, creating a harmony of color in the palette of materials—a spectrum of grays and silvers formed by the zinc, the oak and the concrete used as flooring and as a border to the house, as well as for supports. The architectural form of the cottage is echoed by a neighboring garage that becomes a "child" or echo of the main building.

OPPOSITE **From the owner's office, which is situated to the front of the house and forms part of the main living area, there is a sweeping view through the sheet glazing across the Sussex meadows.** ABOVE RIGHT AND RIGHT **The barn nestles comfortably into the woodlands to the rear, rich in oak trees, and this was part of the reason for cladding the building in oak. At the center of the façade there is a covered veranda, which provides a semi-sheltered alternative dining area for alfresco meals.**

Inside, the house is full of surprises. The materials used—oak, concrete and glass—link neatly with the exterior but spatially the house breaks away from convention. The first floor is more or less openplan (underfloor heating was installed to simplify the interior space further), with the central stairwell dividing kitchen and dining area to one side of the house from the living area to the other, while a suite of utility rooms is tucked away at the back. The stairwell itself rises dramatically all the way up to the cracked roof and integral glazing two floors above, creating a triple-height space right at the heart of the building. Internal windows bring light to two of the bedrooms on the second floor and those hidden away within a further, more modest third level that is at the very top of the house.

"One of the things that I have always been interested in doing is trying to have a sense of constant spatial change and variety when you go through a building," Gorst says. "And when you look at Whithurst from the outside it's a very primary form, so you are not really prepared for the volumetric intricacy and richness inside. You are trying to confound people's expectations of what an interior space might be within the skin of the building. When you set up a repetitive gridded structure, which Whithurst has, what's interesting is then denying that structure and subverting it, otherwise you can end up with very dull architecture. Instead of the building being three windows wide on the front elevation, the central section is surprisingly blanked off [with an inset exterior dining area]. Then when go you around the back of the house there is a lean-to holding the utility rooms. Because the structure is so strong aesthetically you can play with it and push things out."

The house forms a very strong relationship with the surrounding landscape, partly through the choice of materials and also by incorporating the sheet glazing on the first floor. There was also a deliberate decision to make one single plane from the interior floor to the exterior concrete collar to the meadow. Opening up the large sliding glass doors allows you to step between the two at will, but even when they are closed the landscape seems to flood inside the barn and the eye is constantly drawn outward. This high level of transparency also creates a proportional illusion, suggesting that the dimensions of the space might be larger than they are.

FAR LEFT **The central stairwell is multifunctional. It subtly divides the house into different zones, while the skylight above it also makes it a triple-height light source. It brings sunlight deep into the building, including two of the second-floor bedrooms, which have internal windows on to the landings and stairs for this reason.**
LEFT **The fireplace in the main sitting area forms a focus for this largely transparent room without being obtrusive. Furniture mixes new pieces with pieces bought at auction, like the 1960s leather sofa.**

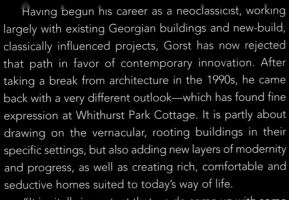

Having begun his career as a neoclassicist, working largely with existing Georgian buildings and new-build, classically influenced projects, Gorst has now rejected that path in favor of contemporary innovation. After taking a break from architecture in the 1990s, he came back with a very different outlook—which has found fine expression at Whithurst Park Cottage. It is partly about drawing on the vernacular, rooting buildings in their specific settings, but also adding new layers of modernity and progress, as well as creating rich, comfortable and seductive homes suited to today's way of life.

"It is vitally important that we do come up with some new architectural forms," says Gorst. "Country houses shouldn't be about control and domination or invested with all the connotations of control that classicism inevitably carries with it. We also need to design houses that are sustainable, with low-energy output, where you can source your building materials locally. All of those are ways in which we can legitimize having new country houses set in a generosity of space."

OPPOSITE **Correlating the floor level to the grassland outside and introducing floor-to-ceiling glazing produces an impression of the meadows and woodland seeping into the building, so that nature becomes the "wallpaper."** ABOVE **Internal windows in two of the second-floor bedrooms allow them to benefit from natural light sourced in the stairwell, without interrupting the oak façade to the more enclosed and private upper storeys of the building.** LEFT **Concrete and oak are juxtaposed; all of the materials are connected tonally and by their simple quality of rawness.**

CHOPPING BOTTOM FARM

"We were entranced by that classic image of a pure, barn shape," say Tony and Anne Vanderwarker, at home in Chopping Bottom Farm, a striking new-build house near Charlottesville. "There's something very satisfying and simple about the form—it's the only man-made structure that really seems comfortable in the landscape. Partly it's to do with time. You associate old barns with agriculture and the past. But the house was also a rebellion against the subdivision of big brick mansions that are not integrated into the landscape and never will be."

It was the look of a barn, then, and the ideal of a farm compound—a house and outbuildings—that the Vanderwarkers were after when they set about building a home for themselves on a tranquil stretch of meadow and farmland in rural Virginia. But they also wanted a contemporary, informal, unpretentious house that suited the way they live rather than struggle to conform to a pattern of life laid down by a traditional house.

Having been tempted by the idea of a new barn house, the Vanderwarkers came across a set of plans for "a people's house" or "dream house" by architect Hugh Newell Jacobsen, published by *Life* magazine, which drew heavily on the vernacular and the look of farm-style buildings. The idea of the *Life* plans was that they could be bought by anyone and adapted to suit a specific site or amended to create a more individual home. The Vanderwarkers turned to Charlottesville architect Jeff Dreyfus to adapt the plans into a new home that met all their needs and was truly custom-made.

"They bought the plans and we sat down and tried to understand what it was that we liked about the design," says Dreyfus, whose work is influenced by vernacular Virginia traditionalism, but with a contemporary imprint. "It was really the simplicity and the straightforwardness of the *Life* house that they liked, so we took that as a point of departure. It helped us really crystallize what we were looking for, which was a stripped-down, clean version of a Virginia farmhouse. By incorporating additional buildings such as the garage/studio and the screen pavilion we were able to create a farm compound with the look of barns and outbuildings and not just a house."

NEAR CHARLOTTESVILLE, VIRGINIA, USA
BY BUSHMAN DREYFUS ARCHITECTS/
HUGH NEWELL JACOBSEN

OPPOSITE **The exterior of the house has the look of an interlinked series of structures with an undulating roof line, like a farm compound.** LEFT **Playing with scale— as in the oversized chimney and the under-sized dormer windows— creates the illusion of a far grander structure.** BELOW LEFT **The glazing strips in the front door echo the steps of the entrance path, situated to the rear of the building.**

THIS PAGE AND OPPOSITE
The main sitting area, dining area and kitchen were designed in a fluid openplan arrangement that benefits from the banks of glazing at the front of the building. The seating zone utilizes the fireplace and double-height ceiling, while the kitchen and dining area sit within a more intimate-feeling single-height section of the house.

As interior designers themselves, the Vanderwarkers are highly design conscious, knew what they wanted out of the building, and were willing not just to collaborate but to experiment, so the evolving design was created around their exact requirements. They had lived for many years in Chicago, where Tony had an advertising agency before moving down to Virginia, and they were devotees of informal, contemporary open spaces and loft-like proportions. Being very active in the local community, especially in conservation causes, they often entertain and Anne is an accomplished cook. Therefore they wanted the heart of the house to be openplan with interrelated kitchen, dining and living spaces so that Anne and Tony could be with their guests as they prepared a meal, not segregated in a separate kitchen.

"Doors are highly overrated," says Tony. "Bathroom and bedroom doors might be useful, but the rest just get in the way so we banished them. Everything is open and every time you turn a corner there is something to look at. We were able to live in another house on the property for two years while the new one was built, so we were

able to get involved in every step of the process and work through all the details. We could walk through the building and think about where we wanted light switches and plug sockets. We called it rehearsing for life."

Constructed largely on one level, the building has as its centerpoint the dramatic open living room with a double-height, barn-like profile and sheets of glazed sliding doors looking out across a slim, unobtrusive swimming pool outside and pastures beyond. Under-scaled windows in the ceiling bring in extra light. Then there is a seamless transition to the kitchen and dining area, although a shift in ceiling height introduces a more intimate feeling to this part of the house. Going down the hallway, past the main entrance at the rear of the house, takes you to the master bedroom and a striking, mostly openplan bathroom, dressing and shower area. Ancillary guest rooms and television areas lie at the rear of the house, beyond and out of the way of the main spaces.

Throughout, the large sections of glazing bestow a large degree of transparency, offering a fluid relationship between inside and out and enhancing the sense of

space. But there are also a number of games played with scale that affect one's perception of the building, making it seem much larger than it is. The church-like windows in the ceiling of the living area are undersized, for instance, but other elements are far larger than standard.

"It's about creating contrasts and playing with scale," says Dreyfus. "Many elements are oversized: we didn't use any standard door heights and went with a ten-foot ceiling height throughout the house. It's ennobling if you can give people a sense of height and spaciousness, as well as views out, even though the rooms in themselves are really not that big. It creates a generosity of space and there's nothing mean about it. But then making the windows in the living-room ceiling smaller than you expect also makes the house seem bigger to the eye."

Beyond the confines of the main house, a covered walkway leads you to a separate barn-like building that has a garage downstairs and Anne's studio above. Another, smaller satellite structure, simply "walled" with screen mesh, is an outdoor dining room, while some distance away from the house Tony has his own writing studio—he is also an author—which draws on the look of a grain silo, with its own viewing platform on an upper level. Landscaping restored the pastures and meadows, which had become overgrown and neglected, and involved planting new trees. But the look was kept very natural and low key, with plots of formal gardening limited to a few small blocks near the house.

With the interiors and furnishings, Anne and Tony wanted to experiment with unusual materials, such as the matting in the hall made of conveyor-belt links or the large screen in the bathroom made of industrial Panelite, but they also wanted to start afresh. They parted with all their existing furniture—while holding on to their collection of artwork and photography—and sourced new pieces for every room, enhancing the feel of a fresh, contemporary but relaxed and unprecious environment.

The collaboration between Bushman Dreyfus and the Vanderwarkers—with Hugh Newell Jacobsen the third, silent collaborator—was so successful that they have since worked on a number of commercial and residential projects together for other clients. The house certainly speaks for itself—a modern, custom-made home that is easy to live with and easy on the eye and on the landscape, drawing on the ideals of the barn and farm compounds, but translating them into something seductive and new.

"Virginia is encumbered by its history and I like to be able to refer to its building forms," says Dreyfus. "But we build so differently now compared to how they built 100 or 200 years ago. How do you keep the connection if you are building in new ways with new materials? It has a lot to do with form and scale, how you set a building in the landscape and how the landscape reacts to the building. We try to design with that in mind. We have a better chance of succeeding this way than if we replicated styles that are nothing to do with the way we are now."

PREVIOUS PAGES: **The summer pavilion is set slightly apart from the house, echoing the main structure with its own barn-style shape. With mosquito screens for windows, the pavilion forms an extra dining lounge that is at once indoors and outdoors.**

OPPOSITE **The large walk-in shower area was designed in wet-room style and lined in Italian mosaic. The semi-translucent panel, which separates off the toilet area, is in a light industrial material called Panelite.** BELOW LEFT AND BELOW **Landscaping has been kept low key, preserving the sense of isolation that can be appreciated from the main house or Tony Vanderwarker's writing studio among the trees.**

CHAPTER THREE

MATERIALS

LEFT The seventeenth-century Mayflower Barn in Buckinghamshire, England, is said to have been made from timbers recycled from the Pilgrim Fathers' ship. BELOW LEFT This beam carving is found in the Pheasant Barn in Kent, England, which has now been converted into a home; another timber bears the date 1734. BELOW RIGHT Restaurant designer Sophie Douglas's spacious kitchen in her converted barn and farm cottage in Somerset.

When the subject of barns comes up, the word "honesty" is never that far behind. The word is used to refer to the simplicity and lack of pretension in barn building, but also to the method of construction and materials. More than most of its contemporaries, the barn wears its heart on its sleeve. With its exposed and naked structure, a barn readily reveals its sturdy nature, organic character and intuitive design to anyone who cares to listen to the stories told by timber, stone and flint.

Timber beams present the rough marks of the axe, adze or saw, as well as residual traces of bark and the occasional carpenter's initials, or a date, carved into the wood. Many old beams are marked with numbers—often Roman numerals—which suggest an early form of prefabrication, with heavy timbers cut and prepared in nearby woodland according to length, size and purpose. The numerals identified every beam as it was carried to the site and pieced together like a jigsaw. As a general rule, the longer the beams, the older the barn, with smaller lengths suggesting the lack of vintage taller trees as woodland was plundered over the centuries.

"What's extraordinary from our point of view," says Elric Endersby of the New Jersey Barn Company, "is the notion that there was this wonderful timber-framing tradition in Europe, but by the time of the settlement of America the great timbers of Europe had been exhausted. When people arrived over here, they found this incredible virgin forest and the only way to make life sustainable was to get as many trees down as possible to farm the sod. We've seen barns with 60-foot and 50-foot timbers. Just as Georgian architecture was transformed by the materials here, so timber framing was revitalized by the wealth of timber and they could do things they couldn't do any longer in Europe."

In the United States and elsewhere, timbers for early barns tended to be by-products of field clearance, locally sourced and crafted in organic, almost subconscious style. It made sense to avoid carting heavy timbers any distance and to use whatever hardwood was most readily available, such as oak, chestnut, elm and ash. There was also a great deal of recycling, and timbers from older, neglected, outdated or disused buildings might be reclaimed to construct new barns. Larger timber beams especially, which could take days or weeks to fashion and transport, were valuable and not to be discarded.

In Britain and other parts of Europe, ship timbers were commonly reused in barn building in the seventeenth and eighteenth centuries. These were, by necessity, long and strong quality timbers, which could be easily adapted to building construction. Some were salvaged from local wrecks, but more often they were bought from ship breakers. Most famously, the *Mayflower*, the ship that transported the first Pilgrim Fathers to America in 1620, was reputedly broken up just a few years later and sold to a farmer who used the timber to build a large barn at Old Jordans in Buckinghamshire, England, which still stands and is now part of a conference centre.

There were three kinds of barn construction: box construction, where the main walls are used to support the whole barn; post and truss—or post and beam—where the internal timber frame takes the roof weight, with the post meeting and supporting the roof beams; or, more rarely, the cruck frame, which was essentially a series of large upside-down "V"s bearing the roof. As far as timber-built barns are concerned, post and beam construction is the most commonplace, with clapboard planking cladding the bones of the frame to form the exterior skin. Horizontal clapboard was used for exteriors from around the sixteenth century, but earlier barns often featured vertical timber planking. Even the joints and pegging can tell a tale, with subtle variations in carpentry found from region to region. Timber pegs and wedges were used to secure the joints between beams, with nails little used until the nineteenth century.

Not all barns, of course, are made of timber. Just as farmers and settlers cleared woodland to make room for field crops, so stones and boulders—which would get in the way of the plough—had to be lifted away as well. This back-breaking work was translated into dry-stone walls and farmhouses, but also into barns. Again, the shorter the distance such heavyweight materials had to be moved, the better, giving rise to a spectrum of stone, boulders and knapped flints used in a multitude of buildings. Such barns tended to be box constructions with thick, solid exterior walls and a timber-framed roof, while additions and lean-tos were often grafted on at will. Like timber with its grain, stone and flint have their own obvious character and colour variations, inset with minerals, seams and fossils, which give them organic strength and tie a building to its surroundings.

Roofing materials, too, had a simple vernacular. There was thatch, timber or slate. Later there were tiles —more common after the eighteenth century—and also tin. Brick box barns also became more common after the eighteenth century, but they could be expensive to build so were usually limited to larger farms and estates. Even in the nineteenth century, architecture remained simple and unembellished. There was no glass, no adornment, no excess and little or no superfluity. Even the painting of timber barns was rooted in practical need. In North America farmers found that a mixture of iron, skimmed milk and lime yielded a hard longlasting red oxide coat —what came to known as "barn red"—which protected the timber cladding and increased its life expectancy. Elsewhere, creosote or pitch gave barn sidings a sultry black covering, which also preserved the woodwork.

"One of the great things about barns is that they might often be made with secondary timbers, but there is nothing superficial about them," says Elric Endersby. "There is a purpose to everything that's there and a real honesty in the structures and a straightforwardness to the materials—whether it is stones from the fields or timber from the forest—and all of that gives incredible integrity to these wonderful buildings."

When it comes to tackling a barn conversion, it is worth remembering that the building blocks one has to work with are raw, simple, organic and unrefined—quite the opposite of many of the more delicate finishes and textures one expects to find in a traditional domestic home, particularly a Georgian or Victorian house. If your taste is for refinement, formality and smooth, polite textures, a barn conversion is never going to suit you. While some conversions have attempted to turn barns into traditional houses featuring many of the above adornments—attempting, in effect, to disguise the true nature of the building with added incongruities such as dado rails and cornicing—these are among the least successful and least creative of projects. The key is to respond to the character of the building, both spatially and in terms of the materials added and interjected, to create a living, functioning and fluid home.

That's not to say that many of the most successful conversions don't mix old and new. One of the greatest allures of a barn conversion, after all, is that it gives you the seductive character and charm of an old building but with many of the tempting services, utilities and indulgences offered by a new house. This means the introduction of many additional materials and elements, from ovens and cooktops to baths and showers, from storage and staircases to heating units and glazing.

But to avoid pastiche and repro clichés, it is best to make a clear and obvious distinction between these new elements and the original structure, while choosing materials that have a sympathetic appeal in terms of their own informality, texture and relative rawness. This might mean using very modern products such as Corian or Tura (a recycled-glass aggregate bound by resin) or more familiar materials, from woods to metals to glass. Part of the beauty of barns is that they are in many ways a blank canvas and do lend themselves to many different interior elements and to experimentation of all kinds.

BELOW These clapboard walls with a raw, distressed paint finish are in the main bedroom at artist Bryan Hunt's barn and studio in the Hamptons, Long Island.
BELOW RIGHT Evans Vettori's stone-built Hopkinson Barn in Lancashire, England features an unusual double-sided fireplace.
RIGHT A monolithic contemporary fireplace dominates the double-height living room in David and Nikki Pike's converted Wiltshire barn, by English architects Pyle Boyd.

As with lofts—the barn's urban cousins—a willingness to experiment can regularly lead designers and converters towards elements that have a light-industrial feel, or even agricultural connotations, and these elements can often have an intrinsic rawness, an unexpected texture or a surprising elegance. Ueli Brauen and Doris Waelchi have integrated a semi-industrial polyurethane, cement and plaster floor into the ground floor of their Swiss barn to powerful effect (see pages 80–7). In Norfolk, English architect Anthony Hudson has used marble chips set in resin for flooring in one of his barn conversions, as well as experimenting with straw-bale infill walls protected with fiberglass sheets (see pages 74–9).

More extreme, perhaps, but particularly dramatic, is the unusual treatment architects Christian Pottgiesser and his wife Sonia Barone have applied to a large mill and mill barn situated near Strasbourg, France. Wishing to respect the original volumes and characteristics of the large double- or triple-height barn complex, Pottgiesser and Barone have introduced a new concrete structure inside the barn—almost a building within a building. It creates a sweeping staircase up to the private spaces beyond the new intervention at second-floor level, as well as an entrance to the living rooms on the first floor. All this is tucked away behind the new façade, which also contains bathrooms on both floors.

This new concrete block not only shows respect for the original volumes and character of the mill barn, it also sets up a number of striking contrasts between the new textured concrete and the old stone walls and rugged timber frame. At the same time, there are plays with sunlight using skylight openings set into the barn roof that produce a sundial effect on markings on the vestibule floor leading to the concrete dwelling block. Here there is also a large fountain, giving the effect of an internal courtyard, set well within the original barn enclave. This structure helps dissolve and confuse the boundaries between outside and in.

In Lech, Austria, hotelier Gerold Schneider and his partner, architect Katia Polletin, lovingly converted a traditional Alpine timber barn into an exhibition space, cultural center and home for artists in residence, and they are also planning to convert the basement into offices for Polletin's architectural practice. Here the creative response has largely been to the character and

OPPOSITE **New and old: concrete and glass contrast with stone and timber in French architects Christian Pottgiesser and Sonia Barone's house, set within part of a large mill barn near Strasbourg.**
RIGHT **Always versatile, timber lends an organic, warm quality to interiors and ties in well with other materials, traditional or contemporary, from steel balustrades to terracotta tiles and sleek stone bathroom floors, in projects by, from the top, Burr & McCallum, James Gorst and Evans Vettori.**

tones of the original timber. A new multifunctional freestanding birch monolith to one side of the barn, just off center, contains a fold-down bed, kitchenette, shower cubicle and storage. Other furniture is also in timber, with a number of striking primitive chairs sculpted from solid wooden blocks. Yet, by way of contrast, the far gable wall of the barn is lined with organic clay bricks with a terracotta coat that allows heat to pass from a heating unit behind. Here the materials are all highly organic and homogeneous, the contrasts subtle, and the effect sophisticated but still raw and simple.

With new-build barn houses, architects have naturally been drawn to an unpretentious and unprecious palette of materials comparable to that which is found in many conversions. These are materials that are suited to the informality and practicality of rural life, while offering texture and tone, variety and visual excitement, as well as many organic ties to the surrounding landscape.

"There is an enormous philosophy attached to materials and the way that they are used," says Swiss-born architect Hans Klaentschi who, with his wife Paula, has built a new barn house in Wiltshire, England. "I love all the things that nobody else wants because they are cheap and have a quality all of their own. We have used things like Russian ring plywood, which most people object to because it has lozenges where the ply has been filled. To me, it's fantastic, with this beautiful random quality. The wooden frame is garbage timber from Sweden. The approach is to do with rubbish in a way, in that rural buildings and barns were always built with rubbish or surplus that people pulled off the land. The difference today is that it's no longer straw and stone, it's the flotsam and jetsam available on the international building materials market."

To Klaentschi, the secret of using cheaper materials and semi-industrial elements, like plastic Five Wall for kitchen units or agricultural green-bay screens as translucent "walls"—or windbreaks—for a loggia, is not to disguise them but to use them out of context and in ways that offer playful surprises. The subtlety and beauty of Klaentschi's Long Barn goes to show that imagination has a major role to play in the design of such buildings. Each and every project on these pages suggests that integrity, along with imagination, is also essential when shaping the way you want to live.

FAR LEFT Timber proves its versatility once again in this Lech barn by Katia Polletin, where a monolithic birch space divider also houses a fold-down desk and bed, as well as concealing a small kitchenette and a shower cubicle.

LEFT In Hans Klaentschi's Long Barn in Wiltshire, the Swiss-born architect explores cheap, everyday materials in unexpected uses and contexts; here the partially open-sided vestibule at one end of the house leads, via the staircase, to his offices. The Swedish timber frame of the building is visible, as well as Russian wall ply.

QUAKER & HALL BARNS

NORFOLK, ENGLAND

BY HUDSON ARCHITECTS

Like so much of the residential work done by Anthony Hudson's London-based practice, Hudson Architects, his conversion of two nineteenth-century Norfolk barns mixes local materials and craftsmanship with a contemporary feeling and a refreshing sense of playfulness. While trying to respect as much of the original structure of the two barns as possible, Hudson has experimented with straw-bale walls, as well as locally sourced oak and flint. Instead of the usual Velux skylights, he has played with traditional glass pantiles, while "frameless" sliding windows make use of motor-trade glazing technology, draught-proofed using car-window seals.

"It is absolutely crucial that whatever we do is not only practical but has an element of fun within it," says Hudson. "And from the outset we wanted to use local materials and people. And the local planners weren't a problem, although we did get representations from the parish council. They thought that straw was not an appropriate material for a house. We thought that was extraordinary when we were talking about a barn."

Hudson's two brick barns—which were converted as holiday-let cottages and are sited a stone's throw from his family's own eighteenth-century farmhouse—do have some elements in common, but each one has been designed with its own personality. The larger of the two, called the Hall Barn, is set on two storeys with four bedrooms, and it would have been a Victorian grain store. Outside, part of the top section of the barn—which would have originally been open sided—is clad in oak, while below on the ground floor are the thick new straw-bale walls, plaster coated on the inside and pierced with a sequence of small windows. A protective translucent fiberglass coating on the outside runs right across bales and windows alike, allowing light to filter into the building but offering extra privacy.

Inside Hall Barn, Hudson has created an openplan sitting and dining room plus kitchen, spanned by a centerpiece "bridge," which allows for a double-height ceiling for these key rooms, while connecting bedrooms and bathrooms to either end of the barn to one another and to the new staircase. This treatment preserves much

OPPOSITE **Looking down at the key living spaces of Hall Barn reveals the openplan arrangement, with areas for sitting and dining, as well as the kitchen at the far end.** ABOVE AND LEFT **The front and rear views of Hall Barn show the clear distinctions made between the old barn and new interventions such as glazing and fireplace, as well as between traditional materials and the more innovative ideas, such as the straw-bale wall.**

tried to keep the whole look fairly simple and again, reduce down the domestic look and keep a strong sense of the character of the barn itself, which was really important, especially from the outside."

Quaker benefits from another "Rice Krispie" floor, but also has painted wooden-clapboard panelling for more of an updated coastal, Norfolk-meets-New England flavor. Oak has been added as a bench-top for a long banquette in the dining area, as well as for the dining table itself, while the seating area is dominated by a freestanding stove, also bought locally. Overall, most of the materials used in the conversion of the two barns were sourced within a five-mile radius—an echo of the era in which the barns would have been built in the first place, using local materials and labor.

Furnishing both barns, on a budget, fell to Hudson's wife Jenny, who project-managed the conversions day to day and also spent the best part of a year stockpiling pieces of furniture, like the Harry Bertoia Diamond chairs and antique beds, bought at auction. As the deadline edged closer for the arrival of the first guests for the barns, the Hudsons decided to fill the remaining gaps through two big buying sprees at Ikea, where they found the sofas, coffee tables and other essentials.

"Barns allow you to be unconventional about your choice of furniture and they don't necessarily require all the set pieces you find in a more normal house," says Hudson. "You can really impose your own style upon it, although we tried to keep the whole look fairly simple."

Outside, at the front of the barns, a series of terraces was created using poured concrete. To the rear there are more informal meadows and uninterrupted views out across the farmland and country landscape beyond. Looking back towards the buildings, the overall shape and texture of the two barns is still very obvious, with contemporary additions clearly delineated. The profile and character of the original structure remains defined.

"We are so poorly provided with different kinds of accommodation, in rural areas especially," says Hudson, "and we get one thing stuffed down our throats, which has been developer- and real estate agent-led repro houses. The barn conversion is a way out of that dilemma. There has been an undersupply of interesting, contemporary accommodation and the barn can provide that. Even poor conversions allow a sense of space and interest."

FAR LEFT The internal courtyard and lightwell of Quaker Barn is roofed with glazed pantiles; the traditional knapped flint of the walls is echoed by the loosely cobbled floor. The bathroom and kitchen feature a slicker use of materials, such as granite and mosaic tiles, yet still retain an organic flavor and color palette.

LEFT Choosing wooden clapboard gives the main living spaces in Quaker Barn more of a coastal, New England flavor. The wood burner warms the space without intruding on the structure of the barn, while the pebble and resin floor adds interest and interior texture.

NOVILLE BARN

NOVILLE, LAUSANNE, SWITZERLAND

BY BRAUEN WAELCHLI ARCHITECTS

wiss architect Ueli Brauen is a farmer's son. He grew up
n a farm in the canton of Bern, and he had a very rural
hildhood. So there is a strong element of going back
o his roots in his decision to convert and restore an
ighteenth-century barn—together with his partner in
fe and work, Doris Waelchli—in the village of Noville,
bout half an hour's drive from Lausanne, which is where
heir architectural practice is based.

"The story of how we found the barn is quite
romantic one," says Brauen. "We were working on a
uilding project in the same area, a few kilometres from
he barn—a farm on Lake Geneva. The mother of our
lient was a painter and in one of her paintings we
appened to see this barn. Doris saw the painting and
he mother said let me show you where it is."

When they went to see the barn, they found that it
vas derelict and in a very poor state, despite its status as
protected building because of its historic value: it is
ne of the few remaining barns of its kind in Switzerland.
supported a distinctive live/work pattern, by which
attle and farmers co-existed in a two-storey space, with
large central void between the two floors where hay
vas thrown down from a hay loft to the cattle below. The
uilding had been abandoned and neglected for over
0 years and had no electricity or drainage. Brauen and
Vaelchli contacted the local authorities, and after two
ears of going through various kinds of bureaucracy and
lanning hoops, they were finally given the barn by the
ommunity on the understanding that it be restored and
ympathetically adapted into a home.

Much of Brauen and Waelchli's work is concerned
vith respecting the context and situation of an individual
uilding and responding accordingly, while drawing on
broad combined frame of reference. Brauen travelled
videly in North Africa before working in Oman and then
t the office of Mario Botta on his return to Switzerland,
efore setting up his own practice in 1988. Waelchli
rained with Herzog & de Meuron, among others, and
as studied in Paris and Barcelona.

"The house is a listed and protected building, so we
vere not free simply to do anything with it," says Brauen.

LEFT AND BELOW LEFT **The
barn sits unobtrusively
within the landscape,
with woodland to the
rear and open fields and
farmland to the front; the
approach to landscaping
and the exteriors has
been to avoid domestic
and formal traits.**
OPPOSITE **The patio, set
just within the old barn
doors, dissolves the
boundaries between
indoors and out and also
acts as a key light source
for the house.**

LEFT **The view from the patio shows the sitting room/library beyond the vast sliding glass doors that can separate the two areas; the patio offers an alternative summer dining room as well as a place for entertaining.**
RIGHT, BELOW AND BELOW RIGHT **The relationship between the downstairs rooms is largely fluid and openplan, with the spaces partially separated by the stairway, fireplace and the glass walls of the patio. Some spaces, such as the kitchen, are double height.**

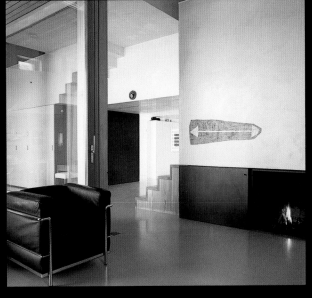

"There are restrictions on what you can and can't do: you shouldn't make openings in the roof and so on. But our own architectural approach went further than that in respecting the building in any case. We pictured the barn as an erratic block—like a glacial object dropped by the ice—sitting in the landscape and we didn't want to destroy it in any way. We didn't want to make any openings in the roofline because we were concerned that this strong character of the house would be lost. In the end we made very few new openings in the exterior structure and all the rest is as it was originally, although we did have to empty the inside of the house because it was all completely ruined."

The thick stone walls of the building were intact, while Brauen and Waelchli were also able to save a large section of the timber-beamed roof, in pine and oak. Inside, the square structure was roughly divided up into three parts on the first floor: a central section where hay carts could be brought in, through and out of the other side of the building; a stable section to one side where cattle were kept; and a living section for the farm workers to the other. Upstairs there would have been another small living area and the hay loft. The architects decided to respect the original partitions of the building and formulated their design accordingly.

Around the main cartway entrance Brauen and Waelchli created a form of loggia, with wooden slatted screens in the old cart doorways providing some sense of separation from the world beyond but still allowing light to filter through. This loggia or patio is gravelled with large sliding glass doors leading you to the main first-floor living spaces. The whole treatment of this area sets up an intentional visual game about whether one is indoors or outdoors or both. As well as dissolving the boundaries between outdoors and in, the loggia, together with the external screen and the internal glass doors, also invites natural light into the barn and forms the main light source for the whole of the house.

Larch wood was used to make the slatted screen and the frames of the giant sliding doors. The tones of the larch wood connect well with the material used to coat the floors at ground level: an industrial-style surface made from a mix of cement, plaster and polyurethane. The polished, reflective surface is intended to bounce and distribute light throughout the space. More partition walls have been made with a form of plasterboard, with an extra layer of plaster on top and then a coat of beeswax. The result is an irregular texture and the appearance of stucco, but at a fraction of the cost.

These materials help unify the first floor, which still consists of little more than three key spaces—kitchen/dining room, living room/library and a guest room/television lounge. All three pivot around the loggia and the staircase yet interrelate and interconnect. The kitchen and living room benefit from the sense of volume provided by the double-height ceiling created by the large central hay-drop void, which also allows light to percolate through the house and plays with one's perceptions of the proportions of the building.

The guest bedroom is located opposite the loggia, with a daybed inset by a window where the secondary cart door would once have been. It is a more enclosed, intimate space, tucked beneath the master bedroom

BELOW AND OPPOSITE **The guest bedroom doubles as a television room, and is opposite the patio, which can be seen through the doors. What is now the daybed and window area used to be a second, large doorway to the barn, which enabled hay carts to pass right through. The folding doors enhance the flexibility of the space.**

upstairs. There is a flexible set of folding concertina MDF doors, designed by Brauen, which can be drawn across to give more privacy, while the larch window screen is also adjustable so that it can be closed up at night.

Upstairs, this sense of volume and space is also very powerful, and solid divisions have been avoided to allow unimpeded appreciation of the timber-framed chamber among the roof beams. Many of the partitions take the form of cupboards and storage blocks, and these were designed to finish just below the purlins, or cross beams, to provide an expanse of roof space and rafters above. An old ventilation gap situated between the exterior walls and the eaves has been filled in with glass, which allows light to percolate through on all sides.

"There's not a lot of light in the house in terms of quantity," says Brauen, "but what there is, is very well distributed. From outside people do expect the house to be very dark, but when they come inside they are astonished by the quality of the light. The trick is to have many small openings, which is exactly what this gap between the wall and the roof gives you."

The floor upstairs—which comprises master bedroom, a study above the loggia and a slim relaxation center overlooking the kitchen—is covered in a darker linoleum, used to contrast with the lower floor and the lighter tones of the timber roof above. The master bedroom features a dramatic triptych of a contemporary Italian four-poster bed, a cow-skin rug and an immense antique mirror propped against one wall. "The gilded mirror is French and it's an antique from a French château that dates from around the same period as the barn," says Brauen. "I like the contrast created between the original architecture of the house, which is so modest, and the sophistication of the mirror and its origins."

The slim relaxation area, with a *chaise-longue* set by a window, is a place to read a book and look out across the landscape, appreciating the solitude of the location. "What really appealed about the house is that sense of place. The landscape is very beautiful—you almost have no other buildings around, which is rare in Switzerland. We are surrounded by fields and farmland and it feels as though the house itself is part of that landscape."

OPPOSITE **A daybed upstairs in a relaxation area offers views out across the fields, as well as being the perfect place for reading; the floors throughout the first floor are in linoleum.** BELOW LEFT AND BELOW **Freestanding storage units delineate the bedroom area without interfering with the original roof beams and the height and expanse of the pavilion roof. Light can percolate up from downstairs through the open void at the center of the barn and filter in through glazing in the old ventilation gap between walls and eaves.**

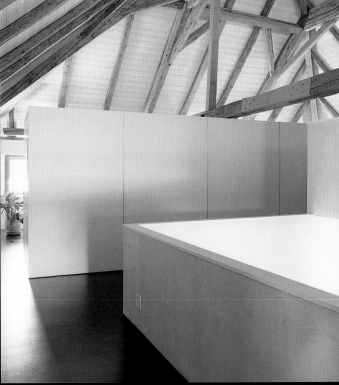

CHAPTER FOUR

LIGHT

Light is a controversial subject. When it comes to barn conversions, light is the most difficult and challenging of themes. It divides architects and planning controllers but makes or breaks a barn house. Who, after all, wants to live their life in a gloomy, underlit space without being able to appreciate fully the volume, proportion, character and texture of their surroundings? Natural light is the key ingredient of a successful conversion and yet the most difficult element of all to get right.

Barns, after all, were never designed with light in mind. These were functional, utilitarian buildings with no glazing and few windows. Openings were designed for ventilation, and hence were small and slim, or used for access, so were large and wide. Either way, they were few and far between, because the point of a barn was to provide shelter and storage, not to open the space up to the elements. If light were needed for threshing or farm work, the doors were thrown open. When they were closed, light was poor, with shafts of sunlight percolating through arrow-slit windows in the stone or brick and sliding through gaps in the clapboard coat.

Planning authorities and many architects argue that slicing domestic-style windows into a barn ruins its appearance and character. They will often also argue that the beautiful, uninterrupted roofline should never be spoiled by skylights and ranks of Velux windows, that a barn's unspoilt roof is part of its intrinsic character. But how, in that case, are you supposed to introduce the light that is essential to appreciate the space for what it is and forms one of the basic necessities of living?

"It is very difficult to get the openings right without ruining a barn," says Anthony Hudson. "It's behind the whole legacy of turning wonderful, grand barns into Wimpey houses and developer-style estate homes. As soon as you put domestic-scale windows into a barn, it becomes a disaster. With barn conversions one of the crucial things is the generosity of space, but the irony is that they can be dark and gloomy, because it is hard to get light in at high levels without having Velux windows and things like that. It really is the biggest constraint."

Hudson's own barn conversions use glass pantiles in the roof—a vernacular feature common to some East Anglian barns and houses—to get some light through, as well as maximizing apertures around the old cart door openings, while also avoiding domestic or traditional windows of any kind. It becomes very clear what is old, what is new, what is original and what is contemporary. There is no pretence or pretension.

English architect Robert Evans, of Evans Vettori, has also worked on a number of contemporary barn conversions, including a recent project at Cotes Farm in Lancashire. The original stone barn had only some small openings, so Evans introduced two big, bold and visibly modern windows, one right at the front of the barn, overlooking the surrounding farmland, and one bay window angled to the dining room and study. "It was conceived as a glass box projecting out of the building, announcing a twenty-first-century use for the building," says Evans. "Introducing light into a barn is an exciting challenge, but the key is to think of the means of admitting daylight almost as 'objects' placed in the barn. Obviously views and the direction of sunlight give you clues as to where the insertions should be made. But to retain the essential barn character, roof lights—which reduce the stark nobility of a barn—are to be avoided and so are domestic window patterns."

Clearly each barn is different, each has a different setting and orientation, and each will lend itself to different solutions. But assessing the existing flow of light into a barn and working out the way light qualities change throughout the day must be the first task. Then it is simply common sense to maximize the openings that already exist, particularly the old cart entrance doors. These are areas that deserve to be glazed in their entirety to optimize the flood of light, being the brightest sources you are likely to have. This may mean having to position your main entrance to the barn elsewhere or integrating glass entrance doors into the old cart way. A number of barns have a double set of cart doors that allowed the hay carts to pass right through the building, and glazing both sets can give a significant degree of transparency and light. In any case, the internal structure of the barn then needs to be oriented around these openings to take advantage of this source of light as it filters and flows into and through the house.

Some conversions have made the basic mistake of filling in the old cart doorways and domesticating them with traditional front doors and window surrounds, which one simply must not do. One catastrophic conversion divided one large barn into two houses, splitting it down

OPPOSITE **In the former chicken coop that connects two converted barns at Bryan Hunt's studio and home in the Hamptons, large sliding glass doors to the rear flood light through the space.**

the center of the old double doorway. The old opening was filled and two traditional domestic doors installed, one on each side. A glorious barn had been turned into two gloomy terraced houses, ruining all sense of proportion and failing to introduce any quality of light.

At the same time, you should maximize any other existing openings within the fabric of the barn and look at extending them where possible. A number of barns would have had secondary entrances and doorways. Stable blocks and cattle sheds would have had uniform openings for livestock and horses. Some barns were largely open sided on one aspect of the building—for easy movement of carts or livestock—which allows a great deal more flexibility when designing the glazing.

Introducing completely new window insertions is always going to be more difficult and a subject of some debate. In many regions there will be restrictions on the nature of any insertions made into the fabric of a barn and planning officers will usually have strong opinions. This is, after all, the outward face of a barn and conveys so much of its visible character. The introduction of

domestic-style windows has been seen by planners as part of the ruinous practice of corrupting barns with incongruities suited to traditional houses that dilute the unique nature and charm of a barn. New insertions need to avoid the regularity and conformity of normal domestic windows, but also respect the original lines and proportions of the barn itself. Getting the balance right is never going to be easy, although one might argue that fewer large openings—which echo, perhaps, the feel of the old cart doors—are better than a sequence of small openings that break up a barn's façade over and over again. Also, it makes sense to delineate clearly between old and new and to avoid pastiche and halfway compromises that will never work. A new window on a barn is always going to be a new window and will never look like a part of the original building. Admitting this and treating any new openings as contemporary insertions has become commonplace.

The roofline, meanwhile, is something that should not be entirely dismissed. Purists may tell you that a barn's roofline is sacrosanct and integral to the overall

OPPOSITE **A bay window in Evans Vettori's Lancashire conversion was conceived as a transparently modern intervention within the old stone building—a glass box projecting outwards into the landscape.**
BELOW LEFT **Skylights, large windows and reflective surfaces bring light right through Bryan Hunt's living room in one of a small complex of converted agricultural buildings.**
BELOW RIGHT **In the dining area another sheet of glass declares its modernity while successfully avoiding the vocabulary of traditional domestic architecture.**

aesthetic. But, on the other hand, getting daylight in from above into the internal living spaces gives the best and most constant form of natural light. And there may be ways to introduce light through the roof that please everyone. Anthony Hudson employed glass pantiles in his Norfolk barn conversions; they are unobtrusive and they do respect the original rooflines. With Catherine Samy's thatched Suffolk barn, Pyle Boyd Architects positioned a large skylight to the rear of the barn's roof, placing it in such a way that it is not outwardly visible to passers-by but is essentially tucked away where—given the situation of the barn—no one would see it but the owners of the barn themselves. Some conversions have also used highly effective ridge glazing—sheets of glass along the very crest or peak of a roof that still respect its profile and form.

Having tried, successfully one hopes, to get daylight into the barn, there is also the business of distributing and maximizing light within the building itself. This connects seamlessly with the nature of openplan living, which not only has an easy informality to it, well suited to modern life, but also allows a free flow of light. As with lofts, light can pass uninterrupted through a barely delineated and largely unpartitioned space. One needs to avoid anything that interrupts or blocks light. Few contemporary barn conversions, for instance, suit traditional curtains, and where privacy is needed blinds or screens seem more appropriate. At the same time, it pays to think about using pale colors and reflective materials—from glass to steel to polished floors—which can bounce and push light around a space.

Private spaces such as bedrooms and bathrooms, as in a loft, can be more problematic. Ideally such spaces need to be provided with their own source of natural light, but where that is not possible it might be worth considering incorporating internal windows or walls that have some degree of transparency—using frosted glass, for instance. Mezzanine levels, balconied rooms and sleeping platforms placed in the overall volume of a double- or triple-height barn allow natural light to percolate around the space while still providing a sense of separation and privacy for these particular areas.

Unlike lofts, barns do have cavernous ceiling voids, reaching right up into the rafters. Without skylights or a sufficient flood of light flowing in through the key openings such as cart door glazing, these dramatic voids can fade into blackness, which risks losing the sense of proportion and space so special to barns. This might lead us to consider artificial light, which should never be seen as taking the place of natural light, but might be able to work with and alongside daylight to illuminate a space and compensate in areas of shadow and gloom.

With artificial lighting—a science in itself—one needs to consider the color and direction of the light source. To create the effect of daylight in the rafters of a barn, for instance, one might choose halogen uplighters, which have a whiter light, closer to natural daylight, than most other kinds of bulb. Yet, more than with other homes, a lighting system with real flexibility is essential. Creating zones of light with a choice of color tones allows you to delineate areas within a large openplan space, such as a barn conversion, with a light switch alone. It also gives you a choice of mood, ambience or atmosphere if you can easily control light; to take it up and down, to take it close to daylight or to bring in the warmer shades of tungsten in the evenings.

With the constraints placed on barn conversions in terms of light by the restrictions imposed by planners in some regions, some people, for whom light is a definite priority, are drawn to the irresistible conclusion that new-build might be preferable to conversion. The quality of light has to be one of the greatest advantages of a new-build over a conversion, whatever one's feelings about the balance between contemporary style and the patina and charm of age within the barn aesthetic. New-build barn houses are, of course, free from many of the limitations—practical and bureaucratic—heaped upon most conversions. James Gorst's Whithurst Park Cottage in West Sussex (see pages 48–55), for instance, introduces glazing around much of the first floor plus a "cracked roof" skylight bringing the sunshine down into the house via a combined lightwell and stairwell.

Light, generally, has become one of the overriding priorities in modern architecture, and barns are not unique, after all, in being challenging in this respect. So many adaptations of period homes also struggle to introduce adequate light levels and free up interiors with more openplan spatial arrangements. The barn presents a particular challenge, but it is one that can be met with imagination, and with style and grace.

London, where they work and where their two daughters go to school, the Samys had long been renting a house in Suffolk, by the coast, where they like to spend the rest of their time. They finally decided they wanted a place of their own and—having realized that getting permission for a rural new-build by the coast was near-impossible—started looking for a barn to convert.

"We used to drive along a nearby road and see this huge tinny-topped barn in the distance, across the fields," says Catherine Samy. "I used to say to Richard that it looked like such a nice barn, but we assumed it belonged to the house next door. Then we were in the local town one day and Richard went into the real estate agent and asked if they had any agricultural buildings. He came running out and down the street waving this piece of paper and saying 'You won't believe it!'"

They went to take a look at the barn, which belonged to the local estate and had most recently seen use as a base for a pony club, and found a very bedraggled-looking building with a rusting corrugated-iron roof,

THIS PAGE **Glazing in the former cart doorways to either side of the barn has created a wealth of light in the heart of the house. Additional glazing in the form of arrow slit windows and a small number of larger openings also helps make the interior of the barn surprisingly light.**
OPPOSITE **The glazed panels in the old cart doorway lead into a large atrium and lightwell that feeds the rest of the house, while long skylights, discreetly positioned within the thatched roof at the rear of the building, also bring in a mass of natural light from above.**

imbers hanging off and trees growing out of it. "I imagine people took one look and said they wouldn't touch it with a bargepole," says Samy. "But when you went in through the old cart doors and looked up it was like this huge upturned ship. It was just beautiful."

Structurally the extraordinary listed frame was in good condition and the Samys' surveyors also found that the barn was sitting on solid, Tudor brick footings, which suggested that a manor house might once have stood on the site but that when it was rebuilt near by the brick pad was used to support the barn. The building itself had mostly been used for storing crops, with two giant sets of doors to either side of the barn to allow carts to pass right through as they dropped off their loads. In Victorian times, one end of the barn had been sectioned off with a timber partition wall and divided into two levels, with animals below and a hay loft above.

The barn came with outline planning permission for not one, but two homes—a division that could have wrecked the character of the building. Having bought the barn, the Samys began working with the architect Geoff Pyle of Pyle Boyd Architects and his associate Ben Kilburn on a new scheme that would better preserve the unity and character of the barn as one large, light, spacious and truly custom-made family home.

"The main thing we talked about was the way we wanted to live," says Samy. "Geoff was a very good listener and every meeting was an inspiration because he would give our thoughts a twist and some stardust. We went through how we envisaged using the space in terms of it being somewhere that could be full of people, but where you could still find a space to go to on your own. The London flat is too small to entertain

OPPOSITE **The sitting room on the second floor benefits from light flooding in from the glazing in the old cart doorways and the lightwell entrance hall, as well as the large skylight in this part of the house.**
ABOVE RIGHT **This end of the living room is partially open ended, forming a** gallery-like connection to the stairwell. Colors are fresh and light to maximize reflective glow. RIGHT **Horizontal versions of arrow-slit windows introduce extra light, as do additional windows in the gable end, which partially expose elements of the barn frame.**

in so we ask people to come up here for the weekend and it was important that people could disappear, read their books and not worry about anyone, or that they can be very much part of things if there's cooking going on or whatever. It's that combination of sociable spaces and being able to go off and be quiet somewhere."

An overall plan for the conversion was conceived, but given the financial commitment the Samys decided to do the work in two phases. Having restored the frame, recladded the barn and thatched the roof, as it would once have been, they respected the existing Victorian division and created a spacious kitchen/dining room downstairs. Upstairs a master bedroom was added with its own mezzanine dressing room making use of the high ceilings, with a semi-open bathroom tucked below. Beyond the partition they also created a guest bedroom on the first floor and a family sitting room above, which took them to the central cart doors that were glazed from floor to eaves on either side. The other half of the barn was completed six years later, by which time Geoff Pyle was working on temporary secondment abroad and the baton was passed to Ben Kilburn, now with Cullum & Nightingale, who project-managed the completion. This time they added another guest room and children's bedroom on the ground floor and a large dramatic main sitting room above that, partially open ended to the central hallway/reception area/lightwell in order to maximize the flow of light.

"One of my main concerns in ending up with a barn was whether we would be able to get enough light through the space—because light is incredibly important to us—without making the windows so obvious that it ends up making the barn look like a normal house," says Samy. "But it has ended up as a space that is absolutely drenched with light, even on quite dull days."

Every possible solution has been used to create such an impressive level of natural light. Two large and long rectangular skylights have been sensitively incorporated in the roof at the rear of the house, leaving the front of the steeply pitched thatched crown untouched. The glazed lightwell formed within the cart doorways has been effectively used to push light into surrounding parts of the house, feeding the first-floor guest rooms to either side through large internal windows as well as the main, semi-open-ended sitting room upstairs

ABOVE AND RIGHT **The openplan dining room and kitchen are positioned underneath the old hay loft; the lower ceiling in this part of the barn creates a more intimate family space.**
OPPOSITE **The use of glass sidings and steel for the stairway and landing avoids blocking out any of the light that floods in through the glazed panels in the atrium hallway. Here the triple-height volume of the original barn can still be appreciated.**

while there is slate above for the roof. On the other hand, you have the clearly contemporary elements, from the flooring, to a floating mezzanine level in steel and glass supporting the main bedroom, to the big sheets of glazing at the front of the barn where the carts would originally have come and gone.

"It is a very simple building," says Montresor, who works and lives with partner Sarah Rogers. "Essentially it's just a big space with two side wings. You would store your haywain in the middle and your smaller wagons in the wings and the original openings on the south wall of the building were just the large doors to move them in and out. It's a very pragmatic building."

A specialist and a consultant in cladding and glazing, Montresor has a better understanding than most of the importance and technicalities of light and its courtship. With the cart barn he introduced sheets of glazing across the full span of the former entrance doors—these now lead into the vast main space—as well as to the secondary barns, which hold a kitchen/dining area to one side and another bedroom/study to the other.

The glazed façade has aluminium louvres outside and aluminium blinds inside, all motorized so that they

ABOVE **Looking down on to the living area of the large central openplan space from the mezzanine level, the pool and herb garden are visible beyond the expansive glazed façade.**

OPPOSITE **Motorized aluminium louvres built into the top half of the wall of glass set within the old cart doors are used to control the amount of light shining through.**

RIGHT **The mezzanine sleeping platform sits within the barn's central hall like a piece of furniture, rather than an enclosed room.**
OPPOSITE **The use of glass for the balcony allows the light to flow uninterrupted, enhanced by the natural sources of skylights and rear window. The frosted glass divider set below the mezzanine partially conceals the entrance hall and front door. Double doors lead through to one of the side wings, while through the single door halfway up the cantilevered stairway lies the bathroom.**

can be easily adjusted to control the amount of light and heat entering the space. The glass has low-emission coatings to reduce heat loss, while just outside the glass frontage there is a water pool, which helps send additional light into the space as well as reflecting the rippling pattern of the water inside the building. Huge glass sliding doors have been integrated into various parts of the façade to increase flexibility and take full advantage of the strong relationship between outside and in established by the transparency of the glass wall.

"The parish council actually wanted us to put stone and smaller windows in the old cart doors, which would really change what the barn was about," says Montresor. "Their main objection was that the new designs looked too agricultural. And here we are in the middle of the countryside living in a cart barn."

Within the building, while the existing structural divisions between the main barn and the side barns have all been respected, any new partitions have been minimized to allow light to flow through the space and to maintain the original proportions of the barn. A mainly openplan arrangement has been supplemented by the addition of a steel-framed mezzanine level, which lies against the north wall of the main barn. The mezzanine forms the master bedroom, while also acting as a canopy over the entrance hall below.

"If you are given a space like this, it seems so wrong to start dividing it up. The idea of the mezzanine is really to create a piece of furniture sitting in the space that we happen to sleep on. You see the object in the space but it's not a subdivision of the barn. That's very important because you can still read the original volume and it still has a resonance of what it used to be," says Montresor.

Clear glass balconies and balustrades for the mezzanine help make it even less intrusive and maximize the free flow of light, as does the opaque glass wall providing partial separation between the entrance hallway and the rest of the barn. An additional small window has been placed just above the bed, with a concealed aluminium frame making it look like little more than a hole in the wall. Two unobtrusive skylights also direct extra light down on to the mezzanine, but they are barely visible from the exterior.

The rest of the interiors veer towards minimalism, with the key textures provided by the stone walls and

timber finishes. The floors are in ash, echoing the old ash tree in the garden, and the wooden boards have a light, reflective sheen as well as being underheated. A wood-burning stove is positioned to one side, with furniture grouped around it. The simplicity of the space combines material elegance and texture with reduced visual clutter, and this is all enriched by the pure quality of light that floods through the space.

Apart from the main cart barn, Montresor and Rogers also found themselves with an old piggery on the site. A few years after the renovation of the cart barn, they decided to reinvent the piggery as an office for their architectural practice, as well as a guest lodge. Ultimately they ended up pulling down the old piggery and designing a new building, but to secure planning permission they needed to follow the size and roof profile of the old structure. Here again light has been treated as one of the key ingredients.

The lodge has been partially subdivided internally into three separate bays, with services such as shower rooms and a kitchenette located in the partitions between the bays. But at the front of the lodge there is an open walkway with a conservatory effect provided by sheet glazing to the front and a glazed, partially transparent roof. As in the main house, flexible louvres are used to control the amount of light coming through, with the glass coated to reflect ultraviolet light and an argon-filled cavity to help insulate the building. Again, there is a pool located outside just beyond the façade.

"The pools set in front of both of the buildings reflect beautiful patterns on the ceilings inside, and it's also about a sense of security as well, like having a moat," says Montresor, "especially if you leave the doors open in the summer. And the water precools the air coming over it and into the building in the summer, an idea that the Moroccans were into centuries ago."

THIS PAGE AND OPPOSITE
The reinvented piggery sits to one side of the garden, to the rear of the main barn, beyond the ash tree. The building forms a flexible space that serves as office or guest lodge, with three bays subdivided by service areas holding a small bathroom and a kitchenette. The glass frontage invites the garden to flood into the building, while the moat-like pool throws ripples of light around the interiors.

CHAPTER FIVE

OPEN SPACES

We have changed the way we live. Over the past 30 years there has been a shift in the way we order our homes, a shift from a formal to an informal way of living, from a restrictive pattern to one that is liberating. The structure of traditional homes has come to seem claustrophobic and frustrating, with a formal dining room that sees little use, a kitchen ill-positioned for access to the dining room and a series of box-like rooms designed to suit one purpose and exclude others. Today we want a more flexible home, with multifunctional rooms to indulge a variety of uses—eating, relaxation, work, play. We do not want to be shut off in the kitchen away from our guests when we prepare a meal; we do not want our bathroom at the other end of the house from our main bedroom.

The growth of loft living opened up a new world of possibilities: large, openplan and multifunctional spaces could also be warm, welcoming and seductive family homes. Echoes of loft life have since been created in countless period homes, especially in cities, where houses and apartments have been reinvented and restructured, with walls removed and partitions torn down to create more fluid spaces with a greater sense of proportion and a better quality of light. From the days of the pioneering Modernists, new-build houses and apartments have also adopted a far more flexible approach, seeking to offer more custom-made, open and intelligent living spaces.

One of the greatest temptations of a barn is that it fits so perfectly into this new spirit of multifunctionality and flexibility. With a barn we are presented with a large open space to mold and shape as we like, to order as we please. The generosity of space and proportion lies behind the allure of a barn and new-build barn houses. Barns invite you beyond conventional ways of treating space; to free yourself from outmoded preconceptions of what particular spaces should and should not be. They allow you to adapt the space according to very individual needs, to choose the balance between open, public space and more intimate, private zones. Some people have to think about the needs of children, others about creating a home office. Barns offer blank space that can be pushed and pulled in many different directions.

The need and desire to preserve the special sense of volume and space within a barn conversion has led to different solutions in terms of ordering and configuring living space. These solutions have been partly dictated by the structure of each barn itself and its limitations, as well as by the ambitions of converters. Most barns have internal structures that give pointers to ordering space, particularly within the bay pattern of timber-framed barns, which can give a visual sense of differentiation within a larger space. Others may already be subdivided by wings or subsidiary spaces that naturally begin to define certain areas within the home. Some may have structural problems, which may actually impose severe limitations on what you do with the space and will demand the advice of an architect and a surveyor from the earliest opportunity. In any case, the principle must be to understand and appreciate the structure of your building and to listen to the suggestions it can give you about ordering space without damaging its intrinsic character. Looking at sources of light will also guide you towards instinctive choices about how to make the most of such valuable resources within the layout of the barn.

The new generation of barn conversions is all about adopting this sympathetic and sensitive approach, rather than demanding that a barn fit with preconceived notions of what a home should be. Within the great majority of modern conversions there is now a welcome ambition to preserve the open spaces of a barn as far as possible and to create a contemporary, multifunctional "room" that generally becomes the main living space of the house, often combining areas for relaxation, eating and an openplan kitchen all in one. Differentiating these areas into various zones has called upon the same skills used in loft conversions and other openplan homes.

"It doesn't actually take too much to define a space in a space," says Andrus Burr, of Burr & McCallum. "Sometimes it can be something as subtle as the way the furniture is placed. But usually there's some other device: a change in the ceiling height, a low wall, a truss that helps give a secondary reading to a large space. It's trying to create certain zones, although there are a lot of more mechanical spaces—closets, utility rooms, bathrooms—that it's good to be able to organize in a more straightforward way and get them tucked away."

Zoning has become an art in itself, energized by the loft revolution. It teaches that to give some sense of separation between different areas of the home you do not need solid partitions that spoil a sense of volume and interrupt light. Without a formal period layout, one

OPPOSITE **Much of the ground floor of Burr & McCallum's Lenox House in Massachusetts is openplan; here the hallway flows into the kitchen, with the main living room off to one side. Changes in ceiling heights and flooring help to delineate the space subtly.**

can get away from hard division and promote connection, with zones for sitting, eating, cooking, and so on. A zone can be created simply by arranging furniture in a group around a fireplace, wood-burning stove or television. A different floor texture also helps visually and mentally define an area and suggest a different function, such as using a heavy-duty material in an area for cooking or dining. Differences in color, texture and artificial light can also help make a zone stand out all the more.

For a stronger distinct sense of separation, a change in floor level—even just a subtle shift—can act as an effective border without disturbing visual connections within the overall shell. Low units, such as bookcases or storage cabinets, can form low walls between different zones, while flexible and portable screens provide another option. Indeed, different kinds of screens and sliding panels or doors can add to the flexibility of space, allowing a choice as to whether to screen off areas or not. They might suit areas that could easily convert into guest rooms, for instance, or work spaces where privacy might be helpful at times. Or play areas, which you might like to screen off in the evenings.

Zoning a kitchen can be a particular challenge. We want to be able to function in the kitchen without being cut off from family or guests, but we do not want the flotsam and jetsam of preparation to be visible as we eat or relax. In openplan barns, as in lofts, the kitchen is usually positioned to one side, sometimes tucked away below a mezzanine, for a sense of enclosure in this utilitarian space. Positioning a kitchen against a wall gives you obvious potential for a good run of units and work surfaces, while a large island can be perfect for a variety of uses. It is functional, in that it is a work surface and will often hold a cooktop or sink, but it also serves as a divider between the kitchen and the rest of the open space around it. At the same time, playing with height levels and additional "dashboard" screens around the top edges of the island can create a way of hiding the mess of cooking from guests or family at the dining table or on the couch.

One may want to look at contentious elements such as fireplaces and staircases within the context of zoning. Both are going to be incongruous and deserve a deft touch. Wood-burning stoves with slimline flues seem more appropriate than big hearths, but the positioning

OPPOSITE AND THIS PAGE
Always in the kitchen: within many conversions, and also in new-build barn-style houses, the kitchen is part and parcel of the main, openplan heartland space of the building. Though often the kitchen will be set off to one side of the main living and entertaining areas, sometimes recessed or partially separated with screens, units, island work stations or semi-span walls, as seen in these projects by—clockwise from top left—David Salmela, Evans Vettori, Pyle Boyd Architects and the New Jersey Barn Company.

of a fireplace or stove will be another indicator of how to order open spaces. Stairs—to galleries, mezzanines and secondary levels—can also be woven into the zoning, acting as semi-structural barriers, and providing a sense of separation between areas with different functions.

Always, one comes back to the subtle and difficult balance between practicality and aesthetics, the goal of an open barn room and the demands of privacy, storage and functionality. Sometimes it is best to think laterally. If you are in danger of packing so much into a vibrant, dramatically proportioned openplan space that you are about to kill it, then look at whether you can expand outwards. Perhaps you can utilize outbuildings or new additions, which might take pressure off the main space, or can you use the basement as an extra service area?

Sometimes it is possible to draw lessons and ideas from new-build barn houses. Architect Michael Sant designed a new barn house at his father's farm, near Middleburg in Virginia, which ties in with and echoes other buildings on the site, as well as sitting naturally within a rural, farmland landscape. The barn needed to hold an office for his father and one for his stepmother, plus a meeting/living room, as well as subsidiary services such as storage, kitchenette, toilet. and so on. The idea was to fit all of this into one large barn room without breaking up the overall volume of the space.

"I wanted an elegantly proportioned rectangular volume, bisected by light and easily divided into three main spaces," says Sant. "The form of the building, with its rectangular plan and gable roof, shares a straightforward utility with the barns and stables and there's an implied pairing of the new building with the original stable near by, which has the same basic shape and centerline."

Sant built his Conference Barn on a platform of under-heated bluestone, using reclaimed columns and trusses from demolished buildings, and created a glazed layer with a multitude of large sliding glass doors and infilled walls above, which also play host to a series of weighted louvred shutters in Douglas fir that can be easily lowered down and over the glazing to provide shade. Sant designed two simple timber monoliths in ply and fir veneer, about 3m (10ft), which sit within the overall space of the barn and respect its overall proportions. These monoliths contain the kitchenette, toilet, storage space and more, easily accessed by a series of doors that recess flush into the units. They effectively divide the barn into the requisite three zones while allowing light to pass over them, people to pass round and the eye to do what it pleases.

Different barns lead to different solutions for the question of zoning. All the best solutions strive to preserve the essential integrity of the open barn.

OPPOSITE **In Sant Architects' Conference Barn in Virginia, two enormous plywood banks—faced with Douglas fir veneer—help subdivide the airy space into three sections, while preserving the overall proportions.**
BELOW LEFT **A partial wall and a change in floor level separate living room and dining area/kitchen in Bryan Hunt's converted barn in the Hamptons.**
BELOW RIGHT **The staircase in Burr & McCallum's Lenox House in Massachusetts in steel and timber is light enough to avoid solid divisions in an openplan section of the home.**

PHEASANT BARN

KENT, ENGLAND

BY CIRCUS ARCHITECTS

The owners of this eighteenth-century timber barn have also adopted the loft life. They already had a London loft apartment—designed, as this barn was, by Circus Architects—but decided that they would like a home in the country as well. Having spent a few years looking for a suitable site for a new-build house without much luck, they finally resolved on converting the Pheasant Barn, which had not only great potential to create a dramatic, openplan home, but also a wonderful location, perched on a hillside at the edge of a Kent village overlooking a winding creek and coastal flatlands.

The main five-bay barn, with the date 1734 carved into one of the elm beams, has a very generous sense of volume, proportion and height, while right alongside was an L-shaped complex of single-storey stables and sheds. This arrangement naturally suggested that more private spaces could be positioned in the low stable block, which now holds a lounge/study, utility rooms and two guest bedrooms, while the main barn could be given more of a free-form, loft-like treatment that preserved, as far as possible, the original drama of the building.

"Keeping the barn open was something that soon emerged as a way forward when we set the client's

LEFT **The barn's original cart doors act as blinders to a vast sash window, with a motorized pulley system to raise the lower expanse of glazing, opening the central aspect of the barn to the garden.**
FAR LEFT AND BELOW LEFT **Views from the two mezzanine platforms, one of them the master bedroom, one a study, which look rather like nests built against two corners of the barn.**
OPPOSITE **The mezzanine structure allows most of the barn still to be read as one great open space.**

equirements against the scale of the volumes we had o work with," says Duncan Chapman of Circus Architects. Being able to use the stables as well, they didn't have all hat much that they needed to put into the barn and the pace was huge. You could put half a dozen bedrooms or more into that barn if you had to; the space is that big. ut we all wanted to keep it open and keep that sense f the overall structure of the barn, maintaining that avernous aspect despite our insertions."

The emerging design introduced two mezzanine latforms—they look rather like nests and resemble leeker versions of the work of swallows or house martins —with balconies looking out over the main volume of the arn. These mezzanines hang within the space but they till allow you to appreciate the overall proportions of ne barn. One contains a study, with the kitchen tucked elow it, while the other forms the master bedroom, with bathroom to one side and a second bedroom and athroom underneath it, down on the first floor. The ositioning of these "nests" in two corners of the barn elped in engineering the platforms so that they can nore or less hang off the original timber frame—with ne addition of only minimal extra supports—while the tairways used to access them are very discreetly ositioned away to the sides of the barn.

Apart from the modest divisions related to the nezzanines and some of the spaces directly below them, ne rest of the barn is left open, with an overriding npression of spatial generosity and freedom. Within ne barn certain areas have been lightly defined, or oned, by shifts in floor level and in the choices of naterials. There is a "talking pit" in molded concrete, which is lowered into the floor in front of a large window o the rear of the house, overlooking the marshes and eek, providing an ideal spot for bird watching. The oncrete has been continued at floor level out towards ne front in this central part of the barn and to the ast sheet-glass window-come-door within the large old art door opening. The lower part of this window can be inched up at the touch of a button, opening the barn o the front garden and creating a veranda-like effect round the old entrance to the building.

"Our approach was that there was such a lot of space o play with and so we could define some areas within but could afford to allow most of the space that's

OPPOSITE **Within the center of the barn deck chairs are positioned to take advantage of the sunlight pouring through the glazed cartway entrance, while a sunken relaxation pit to the rear is the perfect place for bird watching, with views across the creek and marshes to the rear.**
ABOVE AND RIGHT **The dramatic glass-topped dining table spans almost half of the barn, forming an extra length of preparation worktop at the end where it enters the kitchen area, which is positioned underneath one**

left clear of clutter or content," says Chapman. "That approach is partly what gives such added value to the little moments that we have elected to set up, such as the talking pit where you chat and enjoy the view."

The kitchen, positioned in one corner by the main entrance to the barn, accessed via the stable block, is partly differentiated by a change in floor material as well as ceiling height, featuring cork rather than the reclaimed oak used in much of the barn, plus concrete for that central section. Up in the master bedroom, similarly, rubber flooring helps differentiate a dressing area—as well as the enclosed en suite bathroom—from the main sleeping area, which is floored in oak.

A long, sleek glass-topped dining table runs through part of the length of the barn, with the study mezzanine forming a canopy above for part of its span. This table was designed to be a sculptural and ambiguous piece of furniture: an extra slice of kitchen worktop at one end, a dining table at the center—where the floor level shifts up in height for further definition—and then a flexible bar or reading desk at the very far end, where it projects into the central portion of the barn.

"There are quite subtle distinctions between territories and the table is part of the ambiguity of the space," Chapman says. "If you look around there are a variety of formal elements that reverberate with one another. You can see forms and ideas echoing through the space and can make connections between them."

The modernity of these interventions is strikingly obvious, with no confusion between old and new. The architects were anxious to be deferential to the space but to avoid mimicry of the past. The few points of contention with the planning authorities—the barn is listed and protected—concerned the number and shape of windows. There was some debate about the pattern of windows in the stable block, while the architects would also have liked to have introduced a few small roof lights to bring light down from above into the ceiling void especially, but the planners proved anxious to preserve the slab-like intensity of the roof.

The ceiling void can appear quite gloomy at times, yet a good amount of light has been introduced into the barn overall in a variety of fresh ways. As well as the over-scaled "sash window" within the old cart opening and the large window opposite by the talking pit, discreet

ribbon-slit windows have been run down the back of the building between the beams. Openings have also been cut into the gable ends by the kitchen and by the master bedroom and the area leading up to it. Here the wooden frame has been punctuated by light openings and small hatches, which allow a surprising amount of light to filter into the building without at all upsetting the crucial front and rear aspects. Other openings are very modest and unobtrusive, preserving the overall integrity of the building. The old double cart doors have even been preserved, kept open and acting as blinders for the sheet-glass windows between them.

"The standard fare with these conversions is to try to punctuate each structural bay in the envelope with a window," says Chapman. "So the common-or-garden approach for us would have been to have five windows on each side at first floor level, but we've actually introduced windows in a variety of ways which are far more discreet. And even the slit windows help. They all help even if the patterns of light can be quite chaotic. And we also have reflective, bright off-white paintwork for the walls and that helps as well."

Having had plenty of experience of loft conversions in the past, this was the first foray for Circus Architects into working with barns. They do see a link between the two kinds of conversions, with a similar set of principles in play. "But you don't generally get lofts with such a hugely involved and assertive structure as the elm frame was within this barn," Chapman says. "It is a much more involved context that you have to work with."

RIGHT **When the huge sash door is pulled up, this is the ideal place to sit to make the most of the sun pouring in and to enjoy the view of the front garden.**
FAR RIGHT TOP **Glazing to the gable ends of the barn allows the skeletal structure of the barn to become partially visible from the garden, forming a dramatic backdrop to the outdoor dining table.**

FAR RIGHT CENTER AND BOTTOM **The garden has been landscaped in a walled design using planted strips of delicately scented lavender, catmint and hebe interspersed with neat gravel paths and punctuated by taller standard trees. The planting is dissected by duckboard walkways that echo the boardwalks down by the nearby creek.**

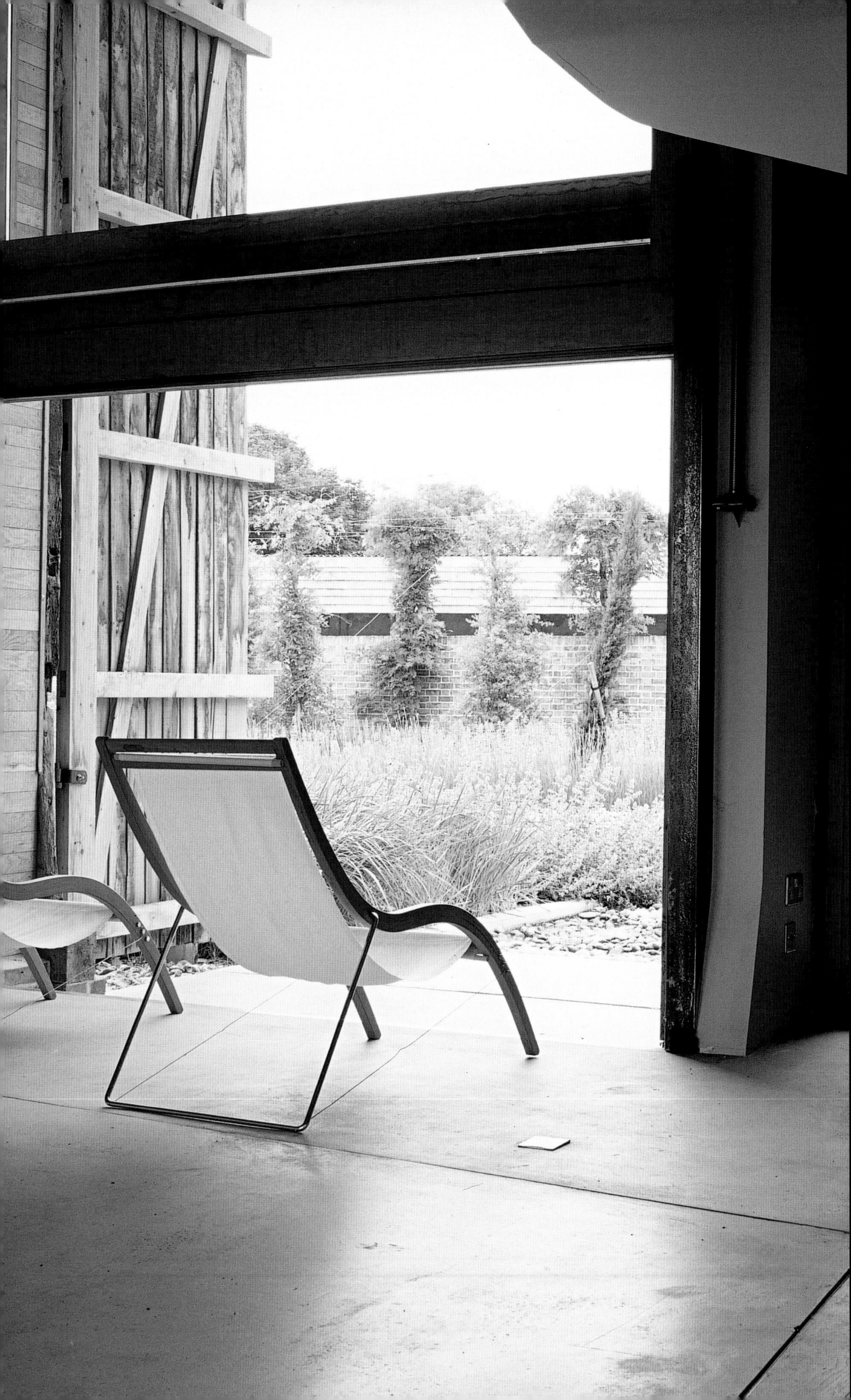

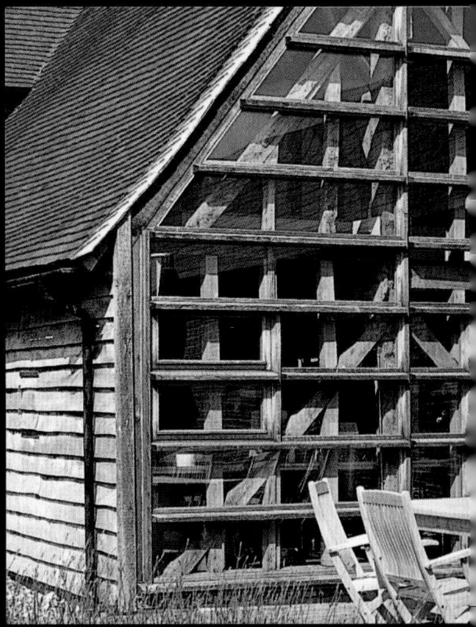

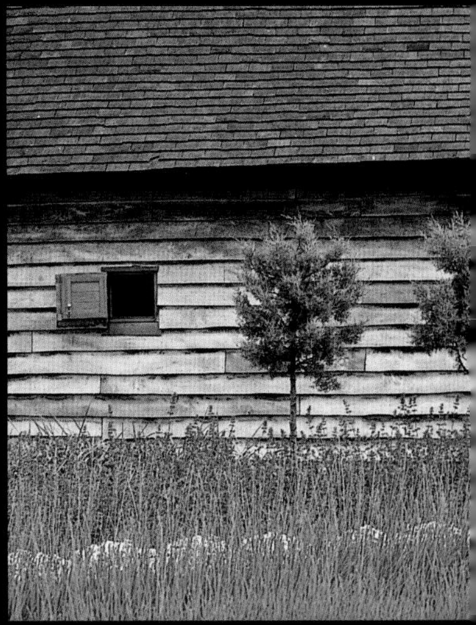

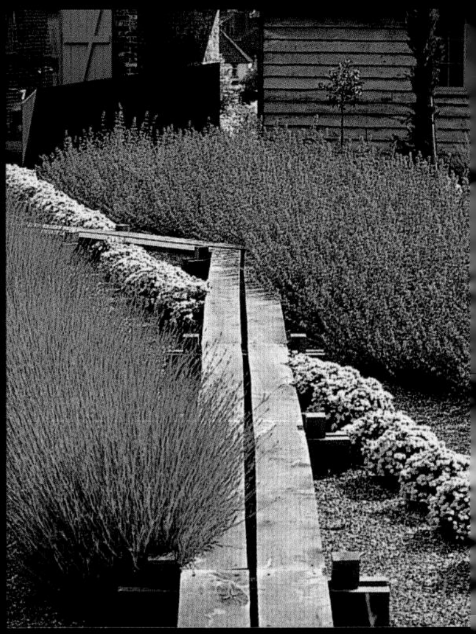

BRIDGEHAMPTON BARN

The Hamptons in Long Island have long been a focus for innovative architecture. They have also seen a positive wealth of barn conversions, as artists and writers have adopted and adapted potato barns, cow sheds and cart barns for use both as studios and as homes (see page 11). Architect Preston Phillips's barn house conversion in Bridgehampton splices both these traditions, creating a home that is decidedly contemporary yet is still very much tied into the whole barn aesthetic.

Phillips's client bought a house made from a post and beam barn that was moved over to the Hamptons from Vermont in the 1970s. "But he wanted to expand the house, as it was quite limiting," says Phillips. "He wanted to create a similar feeling but also something much more urbane—a real modern barn. So we ended up creating a mirror to the original barn with the same footprint and the same profile. The new barn is 16 feet away from the old and then between the two we created connecting spaces like the dining room, which is almost barn-like in itself, but turned in the other direction."

Internally, Phillips worked to preserve the open and generous proportions of the barn house in key parts of the enlarged building, while also providing an ample amount of private space. After walking in through a modest reception area and hallway in the older, front part of the house, the volumes open up as you go, and as you enter the double-height dining room it is flooded with light from a large skylight above. A lightly done glass and steel bridge spans the void above the dining table at second-floor level, discreetly connecting the private aspects of the house at front and back. Through the dining room, one then steps down to a large openplan living room that takes up the whole of the first floor of the new-build barn to the rear, with master bedroom and bathroom above. Yet to one side of the lounge, the ceiling height shifts radically to reveal another double- height space, with impressive banks of windows on two levels and a vast stone fireplace and hearth soaring upwards to the 6m- (20ft-) high roofline.

Much of the layout of the house is left fluid and openplan, taking you on an easy journey through the

BRIDGEHAMPTON, LONG ISLAND, USA
BY PRESTON T. PHILLIPS ARCHITECTS

OPPOSITE **An open-sided glass and steel walkway spans the double-height dining area at the heart of the house, connecting the bedrooms that are sited to the front and rear of the building at second-floor level.**
LEFT **The bridge is just visible above the dining table. The dining area, which is the fulcrum of the house, is enlivened by the bright yellow wall and a painting by Thomas Locher.**
BELOW LEFT **A half-height wall partially separates the sitting room from the dining area, imparting an impression of casual fluidity.**

building as spaces broaden out. But at times they close up again to create more intimate areas for relaxing and escaping. There are very few solid doors or divisions on the first floor—much of it unified by an underheated limed-pine floor—apart from a number of small service rooms to the front of the house. Elsewhere, literal and visual connections between the various spaces and zones have been promoted as far as possible, offering views and vistas to the eye almost wherever one happens to be in the house, while light also percolates and washes through the building from all directions.

The low-level living room is separated into three seating zones, partly by the arrangement of furniture but also by the shifts in ceiling height. One zone revolves around an L-shaped banquette pushed against the low, half-height walls that provide some separation between the living room and the rest of the house. The living room also has a strong sense of connection with the terrace, pool and garden beyond the wide expanse of windows and sliding glass doors to the rear of the house, promoting conversations between outdoors and in. This is reinforced by the use of Pennsylvania bluestone slabs for the floors for the living room and the terrace, smoothing the transition between the two regions.

The central dining-room area has a particular sense of openness and acts as a pivot for the whole house, also functioning as a conduit to the back of the building, a stairwell and a hall-like space that connects to the kitchen to one side and a screened porch to the other via a set of glass sliding doors. This porch or veranda acts as an alternative dining area, connecting more directly to the outside, but in many ways it is also more enclosed and intimate in its proportions. There is also a library/lounge at the front of the house that links to another side of the porch, and this is partially divided from the dining area and the reception hall by a glass

THIS PAGE **As well as very open spaces, such as the double-height section of the main living room, with its two layers of windows, there are also more intimate areas to the house, like the veranda positioned just off the central dining area. These shifts in proportion, height, materials and volume help to define spaces within the house with little need for solid, dividing walls.**
OPPOSITE **The living room itself is zoned into three distinct areas, partly by the shift in ceiling height, but also by the furniture plan.**

The rear elevation of the house shows how the simplicity of the barn form is still visible, but the house has also been opened up with banks of glazing on both levels, creating a fluid relationship between inside and out. At first-floor level the living room spills out onto the terrace via a row of sliding glass doors, while up above the master bedroom opens on to a large balcony overlooking the gardens and pool.

OPPOSITE **The study has sliding glass doors to the veranda, as well as a glass wall separating it from the dining area. It is a more intimate, contained space, with low ceilings, but still maintains links with the rest of the house.**
TOP RIGHT **The entrance porch complements the façade of the original barn building, painted a traditional barn red.**
RIGHT **The kitchen lies to the side of the house and includes a breakfast room within an impressive bay window.**

wall, which allows the room to interact and conjoin with the rest of the house but still provides an area with a sense of enclosure and security.

"I do like the contrast between the cosy spaces and the high ceilings," says Phillips. "You might find 30 or 40 people in this house for cocktails or 16 for dinner and the house absorbs that quite easily. But then there are these more secluded areas like the porch or the breakfast room and a number of places you can eat outside. It's either very quiet or very busy in this house."

The cutsom-made kitchen is a sizable space in itself and incorporates a breakfast area within a large bay window, as well as two separate island units and other steel-topped counters to the sides, and additional pine cabinets. A sense of connection with the living room is suggested by the open double-sided fireplace in the breakfast area, which can be enjoyed in either room.

Upstairs there is a good range of private space, with three well-sized guest rooms to the front of the house and then a large master bedroom, with a generous en suite bathroom to the rear, with a balcony overlooking the outdoor pool. Structurally, the house does well to achieve the balance between this amount of private accommodation and the generosity of an open and well-proportioned space, with solid echoes of the barn look.

Phillips worked on the interior design with New York decorator John Barman, while also collaborating with a lighting designer on a highly flexible system for the house. The furnishings are eclectic, the artwork is modern, but the house itself is distinctly cohesive, partly through the continuation of vernacular references within the new-build part of the house, even if the materials used in either section are rather different. Wooden post and beam becomes steel post and beam; wooden landing becomes glass and steel bridge. The vernacular language is stretched and pulled and the sense of a modern, urbane barn is exactly what has been achieved. But from the front the house still looks very much the barn it once was, painted that distinctive barn red.

"There are a lot of wonderful old barns left in the Hamptons," says Phillips, "and people who are building new homes also love that look, so there's a lot of new construction that has the barn feel, with big open spaces. People really love the freedom of those big open spaces that barns can give you."

CHAPTER SIX

PRIVATE SPACES

We all need to escape. To many, a barn is in itself one of the most escapist and liberating of buildings, offering the freedom of openplan living as well as a rural context and a solid relationship with its surroundings. But allied to this, we need refuge and privacy, we need to feel safe and secure. This is true of bedrooms and bathrooms above all, where we like to be enclosed and protected, swaddled and indulged. We all need a safe haven.

The bedroom is the most personal and precious of spaces. There was a time when bedrooms seemed to be neglected and treated as unimportant and subservient. They were largely utilitarian rooms that were little more than functional, with all the drama of the home reserved for the main public arenas. Now we have realized that bedrooms are actually the soul of our homes, places where we spend a good deal of our home time, even if we happen to be sleeping. They are places where we want to feel comfortable and relaxed, while also being seductive and sensual. At the same time, we like them to be practical, with the bathroom near by and plenty of space for storing clothes, or a separate dressing room.

Bathrooms, too, have been reinvented as rooms in their own right rather than small functional offshoots. We have learnt from hotels, architects and designers that a bathroom should be designed as a room to really enjoy and appreciate, a space in which you want to spend time. As well as baths, showers, and so on, there are sofas and armchairs, dressing tables and sometimes music, wrapped in an enticing package of color and texture.

In barns, where the great allure is wide-open space and the ambition is to preserve that original sense of volume and proportion as far as possible, it is not always easy to square structural priorities with the necessity of creating more intimate retreats such as bedrooms and bathrooms. With barn conversions—and to some extent new-build barn houses—it can be a real challenge to achieve the right balance of public and private space while still respecting and courting the character and integrity of the overall building. In some instances the balancing act can be so fine that simply pushing for an extra bedroom can wreck the whole plan of the house.

Again, one comes back to the point that each barn is different, each lends itself to different solutions, balances and weights. Structurally, the way one approaches a single-storey barn complex will be completely different from the way one handles a double- or triple-height barn. Much might depend on whether you can expand the existing structure to create additional space, thereby taking pressure off the main threshing or cart store floor. Annexes, adjoining buildings and even outbuildings can present a way of introducing bedrooms, bathrooms, guest rooms, home offices and playrooms without corrupting the central glory of a dramatic barn structure. In any event, one often ends up with a home that is unconventional in its layout, as barns regularly invite you to defy conventions and to look beyond them to conjure something more original and more custom-made.

Certain layouts will not suit every taste. With many conversions, one finds bedrooms and bathrooms on different levels and even at times in different parts of the building. For families with young children, that can make life difficult. Two bedrooms in one part of the house, two at the opposite end of the building and three or four young children can render the barn impractical if you want to keep a close eye and ear open at night. For another family it might not be an issue at all. But these are the kinds of structural questions that should be thought through early on, especially when embarking on a conversion project, to make sure that the final layout really suits how you want to live and that the building is molded and shaped according to your own needs.

David and Nikki Pike, for instance, found a large cow shed with an adjoining stable block in Wiltshire. Working with architect Geoff Pyle of Pyle Associates they came up with a design that suited the way they wanted to live with their children, but also made the best use of the building, respecting its proportions and character. The flimsy timber shed was radically reinvented and rebuilt with a wealth of glazing and light. To one end, they maintained a dramatic double-height space, designed around a striking new fireplace, with a mezzanine study incorporating a glass balcony and a partially glazed floor. To the other end they created a single-height kitchen and dining room, with a guest bedroom and bathroom above. The adjoining lower-slung stable block naturally lent itself to the main sequence of family bedrooms and bathrooms, plus a reception hall and a Perspex-coated boot and coat room. The master bedroom has its own claw-foot bath a few steps from the bed, making it a seductive combination of two traditional rooms.

OPPOSITE **The bathroom as haven, as seen in this en suite space off the master bedroom in a converted extended barn by architect Preston T. Phillips in the Hamptons, Long Island.**

OPPOSITE **Exposed stone walls and floorboards give this bedroom in interior designer Sophie Douglas's Somerset home a suitably simple rustic feel, softened by the bed treatment.**
RIGHT The unusual cabin-like dimensions of this timber bedroom in David Salmela's Jones House in Southern Minnesota create a seductive, organic retreat —like a refined treehouse.
BELOW LEFT AND RIGHT **Two bedroom escapes in Alchemy Architects' Spencer Barn, Wisconsin.**

"It was about creating a house that fitted in with the way we wanted to live," says David Pike. "There's quite a lot of circulation space, which makes it feel generous. We could have got another bedroom in where the boot room is but that would have made it quite cramped and not so enjoyable. The pleasure of building a house this way is that you really can plan it for how people live right now. The house has three bathrooms, for instance, and that doesn't feel indulgent—it's just handier."

Elric Endersby and Alexander Greenwood of the New Jersey Barn Company have come up with a number of different strategies within their barn conversions to preserve the integrity and openness of principal spaces while also achieving a good provision of private rooms. With bank barns they make sure they utilize the darker, more enclosed basement level for secondary bedrooms, guest rooms, playrooms and work rooms, as well as service areas. In some instances they have also added completely new bays to a barn to extend the building while preserving the original volume of the open barn.

"We do have a philosophy on barn space, which is to avoid division and to let the barn function as a room," says Alexander Greenwood. "Then we will often add additional construction, like sheds and lean-tos, which will flesh out the barn complex and pull things out of the barn that don't really belong there, like utility rooms or bedrooms. The vast majority of our projects involve an old barn frame for the public part of the house and

then new construction that will be easy to build, but compatible in materials, to house the private rooms."

The New Jersey Barn Company's conversion of a nineteenth-century barn in Hopewell, New Jersey, employed a whole raft of measures to maximize living space while still maintaining that sense of openness in the main barn building. Made of tulip poplar beams, the bank barn was moved ten miles from a clearance site to its current rural location, set amid a meadow of wild flowers and grasses with a fine valley view. It was fitted into the sloping site to take advantage of the original space below the threshing floor that would have been used for sheltering animals. Services are secluded in the basement, with additional rooms also provided. A sympathetically designed lean-to garage and store was added too, plus a two-storey extra structure to the rear, which houses the master bedroom and bathroom and a secondary sitting room. Much of the main barn is openplan, with two mezzanine galleries to either side, and kitchen, study and other rooms neatly tucked below with a dramatic double-height space in between.

Mezzanine levels offer a welcome solution to the provision of private space—usually as a supplement to bedrooms and other enclosed spaces created elsewhere in a barn complex. As demonstrated in the Levine Barn (see pages 24–9) and the Pheasant Barn (see pages 118–23), mezzanines and galleries can be sensitively introduced into a barn without destroying the overall

sense of proportion. These interventions produce semi-private spaces, partly enclosed and partly open. They will not be an ideal solution for everyone, but the partial transparency of these rooms opens up possibilities for providing upstairs living space in large barn structures without blocking out too much light or trapping the eye.

Enclosing second-storey rooms to either end of a main barn yet still leaving a dramatic double-height void at the center can also work very effectively, as in Anthony Hudson's Hall Barn (see page 74–9) or Preston T. Phillips's Bridgehampton Barn (see pages 124–31), where slim unobtrusive bridges link living spaces without blocking the light or breaking up the overall sense of space too severely. In these instances the balance between the ambition of maintaining openness and the necessity of supplying flexible accommodation is weighted a little differently from the case of mezzanine conversions, for example, but the intrinsic character of the building and sense of volume remains successfully intact.

If space is tight and the scope for creating additional space is also limited, perhaps because of restrictions imposed by planning authorities, it is common sense to explore every possibility of utilizing existing buildings and outbuildings—perhaps as guest lodges or home offices—but also of maximizing the private space that is there. A good-sized guest bedroom can happily double as a home office, especially if the provision of storage is good so that the mess of work can easily be tucked away. An enclosed television lounge might also be a playroom, again all the better if toys and books can easily be shelved. Just as the openplan central space of a barn can be multifunctional, so, too, can other spaces.

As we have seen, creating adequate living space can be a real challenge in a barn conversion, or a new-build barn house, where the main impetus naturally takes one towards preserving the integrity of that open threshing floor or vast, empty quarter. Making a home that gets the balance right between public and private space while maintaining the character and charm of the barn itself is never simple. The pleasure comes in seeking out the potential of the space, of molding and shaping it to your desire and to your individual needs. Or, in the case of new-build barn houses, inventing the way you want to live from scratch, following the principles of open living and rugged vernacular aesthetics.

New-build barn-style houses are gradually becoming more common, as it grows ever more difficult to find suitable barns for conversion in some regions. They take on many of the characteristics of the best conversions, while also offering a slightly different kind of liberty in experimentation, structure and materials that can be a real temptation in itself. Just as the increased popularity of lofts helped push urban homes into a new era of openness and light, barns are having the same kind of effect in the country, with lessons for all sorts of new buildings as well as conversions and adaptations.

And there is a growing sense that vintage, character barns are a vital resource that is steadily disappearing. Many have been destroyed, others crumble and some have already been converted. Collectively, this means that an unadulterated country barn, sitting snugly in the landscape, with possibilities for conversion into a very special kind of contemporary home, is gradually becoming more and more of a prize in some countries, as well as increasingly expensive to buy. But if you do come across that golden opportunity, respond to it, be intelligent about it and sympathetic to its character, and—above all—enjoy it for what it is.

OPPOSITE **A small office lies at the end of a row of bedrooms in the old stable block in David and Nikki Pike's Wiltshire barn conversion. Private spaces were positioned in single-storey stables and public spaces in an adjoining double-height barn.**
BELOW **The Granary, which is raised up on mushroom-shaped saddle stones, stands next door to Philip and Angela Traill's Threshing Barn in Surrey. It has been converted into a separate home office.**

THE THRESHING BARN

Philip and Angela Traill's self-propelled conversion of their noble and generously proportioned 1840s barn forms quite a contrast with their previous life in a semi-detached Victorian house in London. They have created a striking and unique new home, bathed in light and blessed with a dramatic amount of wide, open space. But there is also a good provision of private space and inner havens, set within two sculpted blocks to either end of the barn, which become organic forms amid the overall volume of the building without spoiling or detracting from its essential character.

"One of the questions I was asked by the architects at the beginning was, 'What would be the one thing you would want to put in the house when it's finished?'" says Angela Traill, "and I said, 'A piece of sculpture.' What's brilliant is that these new elements of the building have made it into a sculpture in its own right."

To one side of the barn there is a smooth façade to the living block—partly cantilevered and cut away at ground-floor level—hiding bedrooms for the Traills' two daughters at second-floor level, as well as a bathroom and then a guest bedroom right up at the high summit of the barn. To the other side is a more three-dimensional and fluid form. This is an overhanging shape that shelters a carpeted music zone beneath—to one side of the open-plan central void—while enclosing a study on the first floor and then a large elegant master bathroom above and the master bedroom above that. This building within a building has been likened to a wasp's nest or a tree-house, although its form is also reminiscent of a soft

SURREY, ENGLAND

BY DAMIEN BLOWER/

ELSPETH BEARD

ABOVE RIGHT AND RIGHT
The high bold roofline and ceilings allowed the Traills to create blocks of living space within the barn —with their own façades and internal windows— without spoiling the dramatic open void at the center of the building.

OPPOSITE **The bedroom at the top of one of the two blocks of private spaces to either end of the barn benefits from the character roof beams as well as two windows, one vertical and one horizontal, that frame restful views of the village church and green.**

limestone cliff where a stone overhang is created above the sea by the actions of the waves slowly undercutting and eroding the stone over centuries.

Each of these private rooms has its own internal window, overlooking the main barn void, to maintain connections and promote the movement of light. To connect the two structures located to either end of the barn there is a suspended walkway at second-floor level reached via a dramatic helical staircase, which itself becomes another fluid object floating within the striking proportions of the central area of the barn.

"We definitely wanted that huge feeling of space," Angela Traill says. "We probably could have got seven bedrooms into the building, but the whole point was that this is a barn and we wanted to respect its agricultural roots, which meant keeping the central void intact and that sense of scale. If we had put more bedrooms in, it would have destroyed it."

Having decided to leave London for the country, the Traills bought the barn, outbuildings and garden from Philip's parents, who owned a farm in this quiet Surrey village. The location was perfect, as the barn looked towards the village church and surrounding meadow, while other houses were spread out around this central field in a horseshoe formation. But the barn was listed and the area was not only green belt, but also an Area of Outstanding Natural Beauty, which meant that securing planning permission involved many hurdles, including archeological supervision and even submitting plans of the garden and landscaping for approval.

The Traills asked local architect Damien Blower, who used to work with Frank Gehry and now works out of a converted barn himself, to come up with the plans for the conversion of the barn, which dates from the 1840s and is largely timber-framed and clad, but with some use of brick. Project architect Elspeth Beard then oversaw the conversion, with the Traills themselves looking after much of the day-to-day management and pushing the project forward, researching and initiating many ideas of their own in self-build fashion. The Traills lived in a cottage near by while work was going on, while Philip created a home office in the Granary, raised up on saddle stones a pebble's throw from the main barn. Being so near, the Traills were able to keep a close eye on the conversion and make instant decisions.

OPPOSITE **The old cart doorways to either side of the barn have been glazed from floor to eaves, using an irregular pattern of glazing and steel framing, including sliding doors within the formation.** ABOVE AND RIGHT **The walkway connects bedrooms to either end of the barn, including one of the children's bedrooms, which have their own internal windows overlooking the central void.**

PREVIOUS PAGES:
The curving stairway and bridge become dramatic sculptures within the open volumes of the barn.

BELOW LEFT **The kitchen is situated in an old stable block off to the side of the main barn, the two connected by a glass link.**
BELOW RIGHT AND OPPOSITE **The sinuous curves of the staircase are echoed by the "snail" shower in the master bathroom—an organic wet room with walls lined in round mosaic tiles.**

Another outbuilding—an old five-bay cart shed—was converted for use as a double garage and a workshop. An old bull pen-turned-stable block that was almost adjoining the main barn was connected up to it with a glass entrance way and reception area and largely rebuilt, using reclaimed timbers for the roof, as a big kitchen and family breakfast room.

"If we had got the barn without any outbuildings we would have had to situate the kitchen within the shell of the main barn," Angela Traill says, "and for me that would have been too openplan in terms of cooking and so on, and it would have made it look more cluttered. So we are very lucky, because even though we don't have a door or solid division between the main barn and the kitchen it's still nice to keep it separate."

The openplan section of the main barn has been lightly zoned into three areas: the music area beneath the overhang; a dining area partly sheltered by the curving staircase and a sitting area at the heart of the giant room. A good source of natural light has been introduced by glazing the vast cart doorways to either side, incorporating sliding glass doors on one of the sides. The other bank of glazing, towards the staircase, features a special form of capillaried glass that provides a degree of privacy while still allowing the free flow of light. Elsewhere, domestic window patterns have

been avoided in favor of more unconventional triptychs of window light at various points throughout the building.

"When you used to come into the original old barn, there were these wonderful rays of light shining through the timber weather boarding," says Philip Traill. "The architect definitely captured that same quality with the haphazard window pattern, and the beauty of it is that it's not like a standard house with a regular pattern of windows and doors. They have their own individual and collective beauty. And it's not like living in a semi-detached house in London where you had to switch on a light the minute you came in the house."

The bedrooms and bathrooms become sanctuaries within the overall barn void. The master bathroom is a generous and welcoming space in itself, with an organic "snail!" shower, a bath tub and twin sinks. The master bedroom at the top of the barn gains character from the sloping rafters, while a pairing of one broad horizontal and one vertical window offers picture-book views of the church and the meadow outside.

"People have described it as an inner sanctum," says Angela Traill, "because we are separated from what's going on at the other side of the house. With the children, especially, I was worried about that at first, but I can still hear them. And we can also feel that we do have our own private space and can retreat into it."

fleet that was responsible for bringing in much of its wealth. However, given the cost of transporting timber and other building materials over to the island from the mainland, over the centuries barns and other buildings that had fallen into disuse were often torn down and the wood used to build new houses. Now the island is famous—like its neighbor, Martha's Vineyard—as an exclusive summer retreat and vacation haven. And it is here that Eugenie Voorhees makes her home —all year round—in a barn.

For a good 20 years Voorhees lived in a more traditional eighteenth-century Nantucket clapboard house. She works in real estate on the island and one day a letter passed across her desk from a family who wanted to sell their old carriage barn or coach house in Nantucket Town. "I had been walking by it all my life," says Voorhees, "and I called up and said, 'How much do you want for it?' A lot of people do have this romantic idea of living in a barn and what it's all about, and that's what really compelled me to buy this one, and change and also simplify my life at the same time."

OPPOSITE AND THIS PAGE
The exterior of the barn was left almost untouched, with banks of glazing set behind the cart doors, which can easily be opened up or left ajar. The large sliding sheets of glass illuminate the living room, where Hugh Newell Jacobsen created a new fireplace, with window seats to either side and log stores tucked below.

BELOW **A view from the dining room and open staircase, down the hallway and entrance areas to the sitting room. The hallway incorporates closet storage and a small washroom.**
BELOW RIGHT AND OPPOSITE **The dining room is enlivened by Voorhees's library, where the books provide conversation points at dinner or lunch. The dining table, designed by Jacobsen, is supported on a pole that goes through the floor and down into the basement.**

The barn dates back to the 1840s and lay on three levels, built into a gentle bank. Large wooden doors led into the main carriage bays on the first floor, while below in the basement were two stalls for the horses and openings to the rear. Other parts of the building were used to accommodate stable boys and livery men, and there was a hay loft above the carriage bays, with a number of windows added in the 1950s along with a bath and little galley kitchen upstairs.

"The owner's family used to come here and camp out in the summertime, but that was it," says Voorhees. "It was all open board and beams and timbers and what is now the living room, which is where the carriages were, was all lined with pressed tin on the floors, walls and ceilings to keep the mice from eating the carriages."

The existing subdivisions of the barn offered a ready-made structural pattern. In many ways, the volumes of the rooms were more modest than many other barn types, but there was a good sense of proportion to the living room and also to the upstairs level, where the bedrooms and private spaces are concentrated, with

a high-pitched ceiling. As a conservationist who has served on the board of Nantucket preservation societies, Voorhees was anxious to preserve the exterior look of the carriage barn, but inside she wanted to create a very fresh, clean, simple and contemporary interior that took advantage of all available space. She turned to her old friend, architect Hugh Newell Jacobsen, who had worked on Voorhees's last house. Jacobsen's residential work is well known and much respected for enriching the contemporary with a love of the vernacular, drawing on traditional American building types and the simplicity of Shaker craftsmanship and rural architecture.

"I knew it had to be light," says Voorhees. "Something had to be done about the dark pit that it once was and I trusted Hugh to deal with that. I've known him for 30 or 40 years now. He did an apartment in New York for me and my first house in Nantucket. By the time he got to this house I just let him do what he wanted because I knew that I would like whatever he did."

The old carriage bay doors were preserved and treated as part of the exterior features, but behind the

doors a wall of glass was created—with sliding doors—introducing a wealth of light to the new living room. A column support was removed and the overall load redistributed, while Jacobsen himself designed a simple fireplace flanked by window seats with log stores below. Every inch of space is utilized, with closets and a washroom in the hallway, which takes you to the dining room, lined with extensive bookshelves from floor to ceiling. At the center of the room stands a fixed Corian-topped dining table mounted on a steel support that disappears into the basement below. The staircase is a simple sculpture, hugging the walls, with no balustrade and another closet tucked underneath.

"Hugh's work is very clean and so it keeps you neat and tidy," says Voorhees. "The bookshelves are a great example of that and the books don't fall and the shelves don't sag. There is a place for everything and it's a comfortable way of living. He really understands that you have to have a table next to a chair to put your book down on and that you need plenty of closets to store your things. Every bit of space has been utilized."

Upstairs the principal bedrooms are striking in their simplicity and elegance. To maximize the flow of light into the master bedroom, a large glass transom—or rectangular fanlight—runs over the top of the dividing wall and doorway between the two rooms, giving a level of transparency that also allows one better to appreciate the upstairs proportions. Again, the space is simplified and its practicality maximized by built-in pieces such as the wall-mounted bedside tables, the bookshelves and a desk to one side. A high ceiling and a collection of discreet windows flood the room with light, while there is also a wealth of built-in storage and an en suite bathroom. The guest bedroom adopts a similar tone of simplicity, with storage discreetly tucked away, beneath windows for example. Far from being claustrophobic or subsidiary, here the private spaces of the house—rich in height and light—have resonance and drama equal to the more public arenas of the house.

Using white throughout the house unifies the building and simplifies it—a softer take on minimalism perhaps—but also reflects light throughout, especially the shining industrial floor paint, as well as making it feel larger than it really is. "I don't consider it to be harsh or tough to live with," says Voorhees. "Friends walk in

and say, 'How can you live here, it's so cold.' Even my children were a little horrified, as they live very nice lives with real furniture. But I don't see it that way. I don't like stuff; people never know what to get me for Christmas. And I think the books add enough interest and color—it's as though I had chintz on the walls. And once you put people in a room that really takes care of things."

"My wife says it's the best thing I've ever done," says Hugh Newell Jacobsen of the Voorhees barn. "It's the simplicity. You just don't need much more than this; the older I get the more minimal I get." With a marked respect not only for the vernacular, but also for context, like his client Jacobsen was concerned that his work should not upset the exterior character of the building. There was no need to impose a statement on the barn, with its obvious charm, so that freed the architect to focus his attention instead upon creating an interior conversion that suited the building, while at the same time being striking and contemporary.

"Barns all over the world are the most marvellous spaces, always," he says. "And as I like to tell my students, every house should have a 'Wow' moment. People come to that house, walk that short walk up to the front and wonder what those big doors and funny windows are all about. Then they go inside and say 'Wow!' It's certainly a big surprise."

INDEX

DIRECTORY

ALCHEMY ARCHITECTS
550 Vandalia Street # 314,
St. Paul, MN 55114
Tel: 651 647 6650
Fax: 651 647 6633
geo@alchemyarchitects.com
www.alchemyarchitects.com

BARONE POTTGIESSER ARCHITECTS
8, rue du pré aux clercs, f-75007 Paris,
France
Tel/Fax: 011 33 1 56 24 22 28
pottgies@club-internet.fr

ELSPETH BEARD
The Water Tower, Munstead Heath Road,
Godalming, Surrey, GU8 8QE, UK
e.beard@btopenworld.com
www.threshingbarn.co.uk

BONE/LEVINE ARCHITECTS
561 Broadway #8D, New York, NY 10012
Tel: 212 219 1038
Fax: 212 226 8056
jlevine@bonelevine.net
www.bonelevine.net

BRAUEN WAELCHLI ARCHITECTS
8 Place de L'Europe, 1003 Lausanne,
Switzerland
Tel: 011 41 21 312 2266
Fax: 011 41 21 312 2384
mail@bw-arch.ch
www.bw-arch.ch

BURR & MCCALLUM
PO Box 345, 720 Main Street,
Williamstown, MA 01267
Tel: 413 458 2121
Fax: 413 458 2751
info@burrandmccallum.com
www.burrandmccallum.com

BUSHMAN DREYFUS ARCHITECTS
214-A East Main Street, Charlottesville, VA
22902-5232
Tel: 434 295 1936
Fax: 434 297 1436
jd@bdarchitects.com
www.bdarchitects.com

CIRCUS ARCHITECTS
The Foundry, 156 Blackfriars Road,
London, SE1 8EN, UK
Tel: 011 44 20 7953 7322
Fax: 011 44 20 7953 7255
contact@circus-architects.com
www.circus-architects.com

CULLUM & NIGHTINGALE
61 Judd Street, London, WC1H 9QT, UK
Tel: 011 44 20 7383 4466
Fax: 011 44 20 7383 4465
post@cn-architects.co.uk
www.CullumNightingale.com

DAVID SALMELA ARCHITECTS
852 Grandview Avenue, Duluth,
MN 55812
Tel: 218 724 7517
Fax: 218 728 6805
ddsalmela@charter.net

DIETRICH UNTERTRIFALLER
Arlbergstrasse 117, A-6900,
Bregenz, Austria
Tel: 011 43 5574 78888 0
Fax: 011 43 5574 78888 20
arch@dietrich.untertrifaller.com
www.dietrich.untertrifaller.com

EVANS VETTORI ARCHITECTS
The Old Butchers, 76 Rutland Street,
Matlock, Derbyshire, DE4 3GN, UK
Tel: 011 44 1629 760559
Fax: 011 44 1629 760560
mail@evansvettori.co.uk
www.evansvettori.co.uk

**FUSION DESIGN AND ARCHITECTURE
(SOPHIE DOUGLAS)**
4 Risborough Street, London, SE1 0HE, UK
Tel: 011 44 20 7928 9982
Fax: 011 44 20 7928 9994
mail@fusiondna.co.uk
www.fusiondna.co.uk

HEIDE MÜHLFELLNER ARCHITEKTEN
Rupertgasse 4, A-5020, Salzburg, Austria
Tel: 011 43 662 872215 0
Fax: 011 43 662 872215 33
office@kamue.at

HUDSON ARCHITECTS
49–59 Old Street, London, EC1V 9HX, UK
Tel: 011 44 20 7490 3411
Fax: 011 44 20 7490 3412
info@hudsonarchitects.co.uk
www.hudsonarchitects.co.uk

**HUGH NEWELL JACOBSEN
ARCHITECTS**
2529 P Street NW, Washington DC,
VA 20007
Tel: 202 337 5200
Fax: 202 337 3609
simon@hughjacobsen.com
www.hughjacobsen.com

BRYAN HUNT
www.bryanhunt.com

**JAMES D'AURIA ASSOCIATES
ARCHITECTS**
PO Box 2219, Amagansett, NY 11930-2219
Tel: 631 907 3300
Fax: 631 907 3302
architect@jda-architect.com
www.jda-architect.com

JAMES GORST ARCHITECTS
The House of Detention, Clerkenwell
Close, London, EC1R 0AS, UK
Tel: 011 44 20 7336 7140
Fax: 011 44 20 7336 7150
info@jamesgorstarchitects.co.uk
www.jamesgorstarchitects.co.uk

**KLAENTSCHI & KLAENTSCHI
ARCHITECTS**
Long Barn, High Street, Berwick St. James,
Salisbury, Wiltshire, SP3 4TN, UK
Tel: 011 44 1722 790070
Fax: 011 44 1722 790892
k-karchitects@klaentschi.co.uk

MONTRESOR PARTNERSHIP
Wraxall House, North Wraxall, Wiltshire,
SN14 7AD, UK
Tel: 011 44 1225 892193
Fax: 011 44 1225 892193
harry@montresorpartnership.com
www.montresorpartnership.co.uk

THE NEW JERSEY BARN COMPANY
PO Box 702, Princeton, NJ 08542
Tel: 908 782 8896
Fax: 908 782 5345

PRESTON T. PHILLIPS
PO Box 3037, Bridgehampton, NY 11932
Tel: 631 537 1237
Fax: 631 537 5071
info@prestontphillips.com
www.prestontphillips.com

KATIA POLLETIN
394 Tannberg, A6764 Lech, Austria
Tel: 011 43 664 516 7870

PYLE BOYD ARCHITECTS
27 Little Russell Street, London,
WC1A 2HN, UK
Tel: 011 44 20 7242 5055
Fax: 011 44 20 7242 5063
info@pyleboyd.co.uk
www.pyleboyd.co.uk

RODERICK JAMES ARCHITECTS
Seagull House, Dittisham Mill Creek,
Dartmouth, Devon, TQ6 0HZ, UK
Tel: 011 44 1803 722474
Fax: 011 44 1803 722472
admin@roderickjamesarchitects.com
www.carpenteroak.com

SANT ARCHITECTS INC,
1613 Abbot Kinney Boulevard, Venice,
CA 90291
Tel: 310 396 4828
Fax: 310 396 5839
info@santarchitects.com
www.santarchitects.com

STEDMAN BLOWER ARCHITECTS
The Studios, Runfold St. George, Farnham,
Surrey, GU10 1PL, UK
Tel: 011 44 1252 783574
Fax: 011 44 1252 783575
damien@stedmanblower.co.uk
www.stedmanblower.co.uk

PHILIP & ANGELA TRAILL
www.threshingbarn.co.uk

TONY & ANNE VANDERWARKER
Vanderwarker2, Box 670, Keswick, VA,
22947
Tel: 434 295 5235
Fax: 503 212 8452
tvanderwarker@sprintmail.com

ACKNOWLEDGEMENTS

THE PUBLISHERS AND AUTHORS WOULD LIKE TO THANK THE OWNERS, DESIGNERS AND ARCHITECTS OF THE BARNS FEATURED FOR THEIR KINDNESS AND HOSPITALITY: Elric Endersby & Alexander Greenwood & The New Jersey Barn Company, Elspeth Beard, Damien Blower, Ueli Brauen & Doris Waelchli, Andrus Burr, Margaret Chace & family, Duncan Chapman & Nigel Reynolds, James & Jennifer D'Auria, Helmut Dietrich & Much Untertrifaller & Judith Wirthensohn, Sophie Douglas, Jeff Dreyfus, Robert Evans, James Gorst, Chris Hopkinson, Anthony & Jenny Hudson, Bryan Hunt, the Innfeld family, Hugh Newell Jacobsen, Roderick James & Carpenter Oak, Doug & Mary Jones, Ben Kilburn & Cullum & Nightingale, Hans & Paula Klaentschi, Joe Levine & family, Sally Morse-Majewski & Hancock Shaker Village, Harry Montresor & Sarah Rogers, Heide Mühlfellner, Seth Nash & family, David & Nikki Pike, Preston T. Phillips & client, Christian Pottgiesser & Sonia Barone, Geoff Pyle & Pyle Associates, Sandy Rendel, David Salmela, Catherine & Richard Samy, Michael Sant, Roger & Vicki Sant, Gerold Schneider & Katia Polletin, Thad & Sheila Spencer, the Steffen family, Philip & Angela Traill, Paul & Su Vaight, Tony & Anne Vanderwarker, Eugenie Voorhees, Geoffrey Warner.

THE AUTHORS WOULD ALSO LIKE TO THANK THE FOLLOWING FOR THEIR ASSISTANCE: Faith, Florence, Cecily & Noah Bradbury, Daisy Bridgewater, British Airways, Simon Conder, Fabienne Couvert, Liz Elliot, John Finnerty, Marcus Hepworth, Karen Howes, Laura Iloneimi, Alex Michaelis, Elaine Murphy, Jonny Pegg & Curtis Brown, Gregory Phillips, Charlie Sutherland & Charlie Hussey, Jemma Syms, Andrew and Camille de Stempel, Guy Terver, Marie Valensi, Mr Whippet.

AND THANKS TO ALL AT CONRAN OCTOPUS: Lorraine Dickey, Chi Lam, Zia Mattocks, Carl Hodson, Sian Parkhouse, Liz Boyd and Angela Couchman.

SELECT BIBLIOGRAPHY

Eric Arthur & Dudley Witney, *The Barn: A Vanishing Landmark in North America*, McLelland & Stewart Ltd, 1972

Dominic Bradbury, *Loft Style*, Watson Guptill, 2000

Bob Colacello, *Studios by the Sea*, Harry N. Abrams, 2002

Aurora Cuito, *Country Modern*, Loft Publications, 2001

Susan Doubilet & Daralice Boles, *European House Now*, Thames & Hudson, 1999

Elric Endersby, Alexander Greenwood & David Larkin, *Barn: The Art of a Working Building*, Houghton Mifflin Company, 1992

Graham Hughes, *Barns of Rural Britain*, Herbert Press, 1985

Nonie Niesewand, *Converted Spaces*, Conran Octopus, 1998

Paul Oliver, *Dwellings*, Phaidon, 2003

Eric Sloane, *American Barns and Covered Buildings*, Wilfred Funk Inc, 1954

Naomi Stungo, *The New Wood Architecture*, Laurence King, 1998

John Michael Vlach, *Barns*, WW Norton & Co/Library of Congress, 2003.